# The Illustrated Guide to the Racing Barges

### By Rita and Peter Phillips
who have asserted their rights under the Copyright, Designs and Patents Act, 1988 to be identified as authors of this work.

This book is sold subject to the condition that it shall not, by way of trade or otherwise, be lent, resold, hired out, or otherwise circulated without the publisher's prior consent in any form of binding or cover other than that which it is published and without a similar condition being imposed on the subsequent purchaser.

All rights reserved. No part of this publication maybe reproduced, stored in a retrieval system or transmitted in any form whatever, except brief extracts for reviews, without the written permission of the publisher.

**Published by Phillips Design Publishing**
Tollesbury
**phillipsdesignpublishing.co.uk**
© All photographs Copyright Phillips Design unless otherwise stated

CW01151369

Printed by Think Ink of Ipswich
This edition first printed
April 2017

# Contents

| | Page | | Page |
|---|---|---|---|
| Introduction | 3 | Cambria | 62 |
| Forward | 4 | Centaur | 64 |
| What is a Thames sailing barge? | 5 | Cygnet | 66 |
| Origins of the Thames Barge Matches | 6 | Defiance | 68 |
| The Thames sailing barge Championship | 19 | Dinah | 70 |
| | | Lady Daphne | 72 |
| Classes | 12 | Lady of the Lea | 74 |
| The racing barge crew | 15 | Orinoco | 76 |
| What makes a good Skipper? | 16 | Pudge | 78 |
| Sails carried for racing | 17 | Thalatta | 80 |
| What makes a good racing barge? | 18 | Following the Matches | 82 |
| Racing tactics | 20 | Smack racing | 83 |
| The individual Barge Matches | 22 | Acknowledgements and Bibliography | 84 |
| The Racing Barges | 30 | | |
| Adieu | 32 | | |
| Cabby | 34 | | |
| Dawn | 36 | | |
| Edme | 38 | | |
| Marjorie | 40 | | |
| Mirosa | 42 | | |
| Xylonite | 44 | | |
| Ardwina | 46 | | |
| Edith May | 48 | | |
| Greta | 50 | | |
| Melissa | 52 | | |
| Niagara | 54 | | |
| Reminder | 56 | | |
| Repertor | 58 | | |
| Blackthorn | 60 | | |

# Introduction

Welcome to *The illustrated guide to the racing barges* the latest in the *Illustrated Guide* series of books. As with our other publications in this series, we have included as much information as possible for the keen enthusiast while at the same time giving a readable introduction to those enquiring minds delving into the subject for the first time.

The best opportunity to view substantial numbers of the historic Thames sailing barges is when they gather for one of the races or "Matches" which take place each year in the estuaries of Kent, Essex and Suffolk. These Matches, while exciting for those taking part, can however sometimes appear slightly mystifying to the non sailing spectator!

In this publication we throw some light on not only how the Matches originated and are now organised but some of the attributes which go into making a top racing barge and crew. We have also given some indication of the barges which have enjoyed the most success in recent years.

One of the most complex elements of the Thames sailing barge Championship, is the way in which barges are segregated into the "Classes" in which they compete. We have set out as clearly as possible the nature of these Classes and the barges which compete in each one.

For the enthusiast, one of the most interesting aspects of the Barge Matches is to see which barges are attending and to follow their fortunes throughout the race. To assist with their identification we have not only included the usual information such as size, rig, and bob colours but also other features which may help identification at a distance. These features include, the size of the mizzen, hull colour if other than black, location of the davits and any distinctive logos or markings carried on the sails.

For each barge we have included a brief history of that barge together with it's recent racing pedigree. Please note however that, as mentioned in the text, many of the barges have working or other commitments and are not necessarily optimised for racing and their results may reflect this.

The vessels listed in this publication are those which have competed in the last three years and do not necessarily represent an exclusive list of all possible racing barges as other owners may decide to enter one or more Matches in the future. For a full list of active sailing barges, the history and development of the sailing barge and many other interesting features, please see the latest edition of our *Illustrated guide to Thames sailing barges.*

Thames sailing barges were among the "Little ships" which took part in the heroic evacuation of Dunkirk in 1940. Where applicable we have indicated those barges which are officially *Dunkirk Little Ships*.

Finally, we would like to thank those organisations and owners who have helped us in preparing this book. Especial thanks go to Paul Jeffries of Topsail Charters for his technical advice.

*Peter and Rita Phillips*
April 2017

# Forward

As a young child I was taken to Southend Pier in the mid 1960s to see the first of the newly revived barge matches. While my Grandfather reminisced with his contemporaries I watched the spectacle unaware how much a part of my life barges would become. I am sure my grandfathers generation thought they were witnessing the end of an era in fact it was just the beginning, as barges ,after a hard working life entered a semi retirement as charter barges, school ships and yachts.

As interest grew in preserving barges so more races were organised and these races did as much to raise the profile of sailing barges as the earliest matches a hundred years earlier. Thankfully interest and enthusiasm continues to fuel this renaissance and the races are a central part of our coastal scene showcasing these majestic craft and the skills needed to sail them.

There is little doubt that this spectacle will continue to enthrall for years to come and I hope it will encourage today's spectators to do what they can to help barges sail into the future.

Paul Jeffries (Topsail Charters)

## What is a Thames sailing barge?

For the purposes of this book, a Thames sailing barge is any vessel accepted by the Sailing Barge Association for entry into their Thames sailing barge races or "Matches" as they are referred to.

In practice this means those surviving box like, flat bottomed cargo carrying craft with lee boards which have evolved around the Thames Estuary and have a design peculiar to that area. This includes barges big and small built to work as cargo carriers in their hay day of the late Nineteenth and early Twentieth Centuries. It also includes contemporary or later vessels built to similar design but intended solely for pleasure use from the start - "Barge Yachts".

Lighters and barges have been seen on the River Thames from before the middle ages. It was with the expansion of London and particularly the Port of London in the Eighteenth Century, that a gradual change from the medieval Hoy to sailing barges took place. The paintings of *Samuel Scott* and *Canaletto* now provide us with an interesting insight into the various types of shipping to be found on the Thames at this time.

The shallow draft, shovel ended, simple design of these early barges gave them an advantage over the heavier more complex Hoys when coastal trade expanded, particularly when navigating the shallow estuaries and creeks of East Anglia and Kent where their flat bottoms were ideal.

The early single masted spritsail rigged vessels evolved in size and form. Bow and stern shapes developed from a flat lighter like shape through sloping "snib" bows to the transom sterns and vertical stems we see today. As barges increased in size to take ever growing cargoes, Mizzen masts were added to aid directional stability and, from the late Nineteenth Century, wheels began to replace long and cumbersome tillers especially on the larger barges.

By the end of the Nineteenth Century payloads of up to 200 tons of every type of cargo imaginable were being carried. Coal from the North East, chemicals from the EDME factory at Mistley and grain for the brewers and maltster's throughout the region, Brick makers and gunpowder mills operated their own fleets of barges. Tiny barges like *Cygnet* worked the narrow waterways to reach isolated farms. From these farms came straw and grain for the horses London relied on for transport. Return trips were made with horse manure for use as fertiliser. Barges designed to carry bricks or hay and straw were proportionally wider and known as "Brickies" or "Stackies" respectively.

The Thames barge continued it's evolution, metal hulls, lighter than wood and without the need for internal bracing were able to carry more cargo for a given size and weight. In time sails were augmented by, then replaced with, engines. Whatever their refinements however, competition from road and rail meant that by the 1960's the sailing barge was no longer commercially viable.

Fortunately both the use and equipment of the barges is still evolving, some are fitted out for corporate use while others are equipped for educational work. A number earn their living as charter barges, still others purely as pleasure craft.

All the barges featured in this book are owned and operated by Charities, Companies or individuals who share a passion for not only preserving our maritime history but keeping it alive by sailing it.

# Origins of the Thames Barge Matches

Henry Dodd has two claims to fame. The first that he is believed to have been the prototype for Charles Dickens character Mr Boffin, the wealthy "Golden Dustman" of the novel *Our mutual friend*, is of little concern to us here. The second, that he organised the first official race or "Match" between Thames sailing barges had not only a fundamental effect on the future history of the barges but is the reason so many enjoy the level of publicity they do today.

In his book *Sailing Barges* Frank Carr states, "*The Golden age of the barge did not really begin until the year 1863, when in the fertile brain of a Mr. Henry Dodd was born the idea that has done more than anything else to improve the build of the barges and to raise the status of the bargemen. For in that year the Annual Barge Sailing Match was founded by him and his friends on the Corn Exchange. The innovation was an immediate success, and as early as 1874 barges were being built specially for the race.*"

Born in 1801 at Hackney, Henry Dodd, like the fictional "Golden Dustman" (a soubriquet now firmly linked to Dodd himself) made his fortune from London's rubbish. His business started with the collection and removal of this refuse, possibly even as a lowly "Scavenger", searching for items which could be sold for a profit. Apparently prospering, Dodd soon concluded that he could make more money transporting waste to the works along the Thames which burned it and used the resulting ash in brick making.

From using horse drawn carts, Henry Dodd's enterprise expanded to include a small fleet of sailing barges and later still he was able to replace or augment his original second hand fleet with new barges. Further expansion followed with the acquisition of brick making factories of his own. Dodd's growing wealth of course meant growing respectability despite his humble origins. He became a City Liveryman and a member of the Metropolitan Board of Works. He also became a Patron of the London theatre scene and it is through this interest that he met and shared a friendship with Charles Dickens and came to inspire the character of "Mr Boffin".

As a barge owner, Dodd had a vested interest in improving the performance and reputation of the Thames barges. The behavior of some crews at the time leaving a certain amount to be desired in respect of the latter! However leisurely the progress of a Thames barge under sail may appear today, "In trade" time was money. Many cargoes were had on a first come, first served basis and the expression "Racing for turn" referred to competition to be first in the queue for available work.

It was against this background that Henry Dodd and some like minded individuals came up with the idea of promoting the racing of barges to stimulate their design, reputation and performance. Thus it was that in 1863, with the help of the "Prince of Wales Yacht Club" Committee, Henry Dodd organised the first official Thames sailing barge race or "Match". The course decided upon was from Gravesend in Kent to the Nore Light and back.

The Nore Light was at this time, a light ship, approximately 4 miles South East of Shoebury, warning of the Nore sandbank, both a landmark and a hazard where the Thames meets the North Sea. The last lightship was withdrawn during the First World War and the site is now marked by *Sea Reach No.1 Buoy*.

A stipulation in the rules, one which remains to this day, was that no barge should carry a working crew of more than five. There were also stipulations as to the sails which could be carried (four - Jib, Main, Fore and Mizzen) and stipulating that one sweep (Oar) could be used to avoid a collision.

Some sources have it that the *Prince of Wales Yacht Club* under who's flag this first race took place, rather than enjoying Royal patronage, took it's name from the *Prince of Wales* Public House, probably the one in Avenue Road Erith. This theory is supported by the lack of information available on such an organisation save for an entry in the *British yacht club and sailing club* index showing a red burgee with crown and prince of Wales feathers as belonging to the Club in the 1860s. This listing is under the section dealing with clubs which no longer exist. We have been unable to find any other record of the Club.

Generous prizes in the form of cash, plate and Spode were donated for this first Match which might account for both the number of entries and the considerable press interest.

Eight barges contested the Match which was held on 26 August. Positions with finishing times were as follows:

| *W H D* | Skipper *Harry Munns* | 6h 55m 30s |
|---|---|---|
| *Mary* | " *T Walker* | 7h 4m 55s |
| *Claude* | " *T Bradley* | 7h 12m 31s |
| *James* | " *J Robinson* | 7h 18m 30s |
| *Alice* | Not timed at finish | |
| *Eliza* | Not timed at finish | |
| *Emma* | Not timed at finish | |
| *Queen Caroline* | Not timed at finish | |

*W H D* was a 40 ton barge registered No. 9076 of London, built in 1853, and owned by Henry Dodd! She had an adventurous life having several owners, being re named *Josaphine* and being re built at Faversham in 1892. She was run down and sunk in the Thames in 1890 to be raised and rebuilt again. She was finally broken up in 1912.

*Claud* was possibly the 36 ton Spritsail barge No. 17556 built in 1856 appearing in the ownership of Robert Dodd of Faversham in the Merchant Navy List of 1893.

*James* is listed as *James Robinson*, No. 6153 of 21 ton owned by J J Robinson of Northfleet.

*W H D, Eliza, James* and *Emma* were "Swim headed" barges, with a flat bow profile similar to a lighter. The remainder were the stem headed barges we are familiar with today.

The event continued to grow and it's organisation subsequently passed to a committee of barge owners. Within ten years barges were being specially built to win the race and Matches were followed by passenger steamers carrying up to 10,000 spectators. On his death in 1881 Henry Dodd's charitable bequests included £5000 to the *Worshipful Company of Fishmongers* to be invested so that the annual income could be used to fund cups to be awarded as prizes in

Barge Matches and to provide for the welfare of Bargemen falling on hard times.

Until 1910 the Company funded two silver cups to be awarded as prizes, the fund was then used solely to provide pensions for bargemen for a number of years. Since 1998 Pennants for the Blackwater Match have also been funded.

The connection with Charles Dickens was to continue, as in the latter years of the Nineteenth century, his son, also Charles, chronicled ensuing Matches in his annual gazetteer.

From this early beginning the popularity of races for barges grew with contests being held on many of the rivers round the coast in the vicinity of the Thames estuary. It was not long before barges were being built with the winning of Matches in mind.

*Please note:*

*We have referred extensively to Chris Kite's superb article "The great sailing barge race" in "Mainsheet", the magazine for the Society for Sailing Barge Research, Autumn 2016 edition. This article also includes a detailed account of the first Match. Chris has also kindly updated some of the information contained in that article.*

# The Thames sailing barge Championship

Races, traditionally called "Matches", for Thames sailing barges are organised by local Clubs and Committees and make up the Sailing Barge Championship sponsored by the Sailing Barge Association. The results of the Seven major Matches are used to calculate the Champion Barge for the year, over all and in each Class.

In addition to the Championship Matches, there is usually a race between Gravesend and Harwich, "The Passage Match" and a race for barges and traditional craft at the *Whitstable Harbour Regatta* in August.

Points are awarded for the Championship events. Each barge "Discards" its lowest points score if it competes in all the Matches.

Full details of how points and classes are allocated can be found on the web site of the S B A - *www.sailingbargeassociation.co.uk*

In brief points are usually awarded as follows;
1 Point for each barge starting.
1 Point for each barge finishing.
3, 2, and 1 Point respectively for first, second and third in Class finishers.
1 Point for fastest start in Class.
1 Point for fastest start overall.
1 Point for first past outer marker.
Additional points can be awarded for seamanship.

Ten and five minute warning guns are fired before the starting gun. The prize for the fastest start in each Class going to the barge which crosses the start line first after the Start Gun has been fired.

Except for the Passage Match, which starts at Gravesend and finishes at Harwich, matches are usually raced down river, round one or more buoys and back. In the case of the Southend Match this is often in the form of a figure eight. thus virtually the whole race can be seen from the end of the Pier.

The exact course for each event is decided by the Match Committee taking into account weather conditions on the day. Start times are set to allow barges to sail out on the ebb tide and back on the flood tide.

Race Committees make a decision on the length of the course and hence duration of the Match on the day, based on the conditions currently prevailing. (The Pin Mill Match for instance, has the option of approximately twenty courses to chose from.) Should conditions change during a race, Match Committees can shorten the course to ensure that all barges are able to return with the tide as planned.

Although all the Barge Matches are independently organised, they are coordinated so as to prevent clashes and to give a fairly even spacing of events throughout the season. The Blackwater Match is the most limited for suitable tide dates, and is therefore the one around which the calendar is based.

The Passage Match no longer counts towards the Championship and indeed has not been held recently, (Though it is scheduled for 2017) It now acts solely as a feeder for the Pin Mill event. Barges make their way up river at the end of the race and are therefore in position ready for the Pin Mill Match held on the next Saturday.

From 2015 each Class has been scored separately with a Champion Barge in each Class, with an overall Champion Barge based on the greatest number of points scored across the Classes.

Prior to 2015, although points were scored for finishing positions within Class, these were aggregated to give an overall Championship position only.

At first sight it may appear that a points system based on an average score over the number of events competed may give a more accurate reflection of the racing capabilities of the barges concerned. However the present system, clearly favouring those who enter the most Matches, justly rewards the immense investment of both time and money involved in taking part.

When considering the number of entries shown for each barge, it should be remembered that the several days which it can take for a barge and crew to travel to a Match, compete and return to base, not only incur expense in themselves but in the case of a charter barge or even a Charity operated one, represent days on which they are not earning their living.

Some barge operators seek to defray some of their expenses by carrying paying passengers during Matches, either when competing or "Following" acting as floating grandstands.

**Barge Match numbers**

In the following table we have listed the number of barges competing in the Matches which make up the Barge Match Championship in the three years leading up to 2017.

Please note that this is for information only as past numbers attending do not guarantee a similar level of participation in the future. In particular, the weather can make a big difference to the number of barges competing In a Match. The 2015 Blackwater event for example was badly affected by high winds with only two barges making a late start in an attempt to put on some form of race. Bad weather on the days preceding a Match can also have an adverse effect on numbers as barges may find it impossible or unsafe to make the necessary journeys to attend.

| Match | Number of barges competing | | |
|---|---|---|---|
| | 2016 | 2015 | 2014 |
| Medway | 10 | 10 | 8 |
| Thames | 8 | 10 | Not contested |
| Pin Mill | 13 | 9 | 12 |
| Colne | 6 | 8 | 8 |
| Swale | 8 | 8 | 8 |
| Southend | 7 | 6 | 11 |
| Blackwater | 11 | 2 | 12 |

## Results 2016

The following are the results in the various Classes contested in 2016 as listed by the Sailing Barge Association-

### Bowsprit class

1st *Edme* 30 points from 5 starts
2nd *Marjorie* 19 points from 5 starts
3rd *Mirosa* 18 points from 3 starts
4th *Xylonite* 17 points from 4 starts
5th *Adieu* 13 points from 4 starts
6th *Dawn* 4 points from 1 start

### Fast staysail Class

1st *Niagara* 38 points from 7 starts
2nd *Edith May* 25 points from 5 starts
3rd *Melissa* 11 points from 3 starts and *Repertor* 11 points from 4 starts
5th *Reminder* 7 points from 3 starts
6th *Ardwina* 4 points from 1 start

### Slow Staysail/Coasting class

1st *Lady of the Lea* 20 points from 4 starts
2nd *Cambria* 12 points from 2 starts and *Pudge* 12 points from 3 starts
4th *Centaur* 11 points from 4 starts
5th *Blackthorn* 6 points from 2 starts and *Cygnet* 6 points from 1 start
7th *Defiance* and *Orinoco* 4 points from 1 start each

### Overall Championship

By aggregating the points scored in their respective classes we arrive at the following positions-

1st *Niagara*
2nd *Edme*
3rd *Edith May*
4th *Lady of the Lea*
5th *Marjorie*
6th *Mirosa*
7th *Xylonite*
8th *Adieu*
9th *Cambria* and *Pudge*
11th *Centaur, Melissa* and *Repertor*
14th *Reminder*
15th *Blackthorn* and *Cygnet*
17th *Ardwina, Dawn, Defiance* and *Orinoco*

# Classes

For the purposes of the Sailing Barge Association Championship, barges race in "Classes" based partly on their sail plans and partly on their speed potential. The barge with the most points in each class becomes the "Champion Barge" for that class for the season.

Below we have set out, with diagrams, the classes recognised by the S B A for Championship purposes. The S B A Award Trophies for the Champion Barge in each of these classes together with the trophy for the over all "Champion Barge". Please note however that each of the Barge Match Committees set their own designations for classes which although broadly following the S B A designations, do vary in detail, e.g. Pin Mill has Classes *A B C*. The Thames Match *Champion Bowsprit, Champion Staysail* and *Coasting*. Other Matches have their own permutations while still complying in principle with the Championship Groupings.

The Championship Classes are -

*Bowsprit*

For bowsprit rigged barges. In general these barges are smaller than the big "Coasting " barges and usually carry the spritsail rig on both main and mizzen masts. Bowsprit barges can race in the Staysail class if they raise their bowsprits. Although not a common occurrence, this does happen occasionally either to make the Staysail Class more competitive or simply at the whim of the owner.

*Spritsail Barge, Bowsprit Rig*

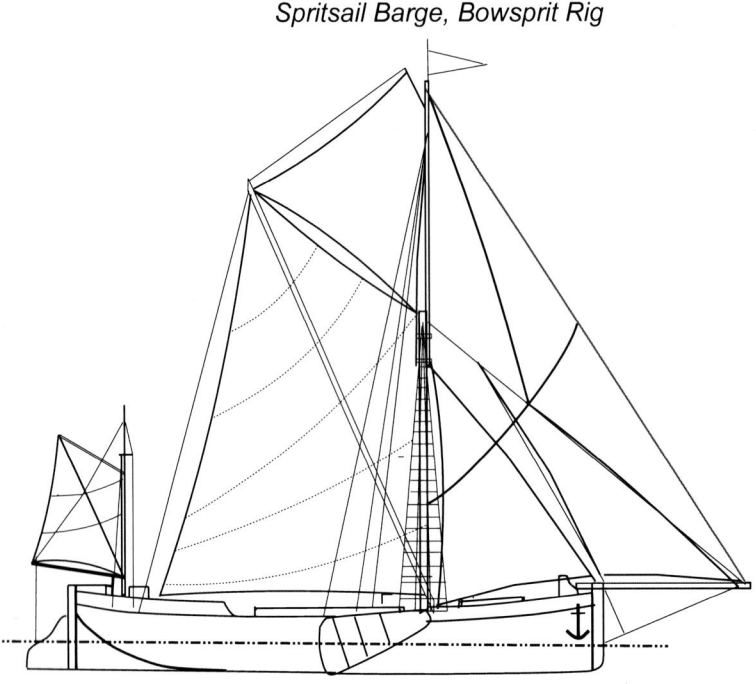

*Fast Staysail*

Staysail barges are those which race without a bowsprit. In trade this rig was particularly convenient when working in confined spaces such as busy ports and harbours. The price for this convenience is the slight reduction of the sail area which can be carried and hence of potential speed.

The *Fast Staysail* Class consists of those barges considered by the S B A to represent the quickest of the type.

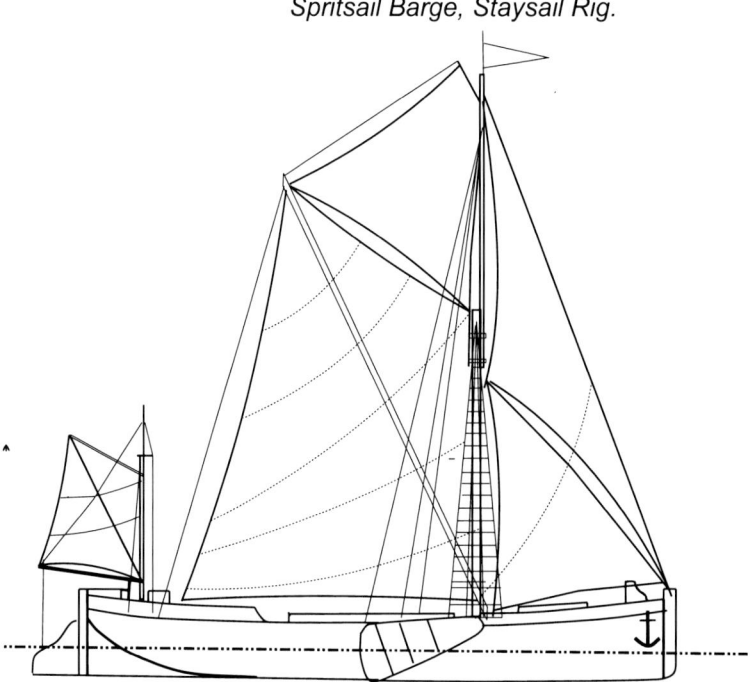

*Spritsail Barge, Staysail Rig.*

*Slow Staysail/Coasting*

This is something of a "Catch all" class, encompassing those barges which cannot be fairly or competitively included in the other classes. Staysail barges which are not considered to be quick enough to compete with the fast metal barges such as *Niagara* and *Reminder* find themselves in this class as do the big 90 foot plus Mulie rig Coasters such as *Cambria* and *Thalatta*.

This class also accommodates some of the smaller working barges such as *Cygnet* and *Lady of the Lea* and barge yachts such as *Dinah* and *Blackthorn* which would not fit into the other classes.

However strange the make up of this class can appear at times, it does seem to give a balanced set of results and represents as fair a basis for racing such a varied collection of vessels as can reasonably be expected.

*Coasting Barge, "Mulie" Rig.*

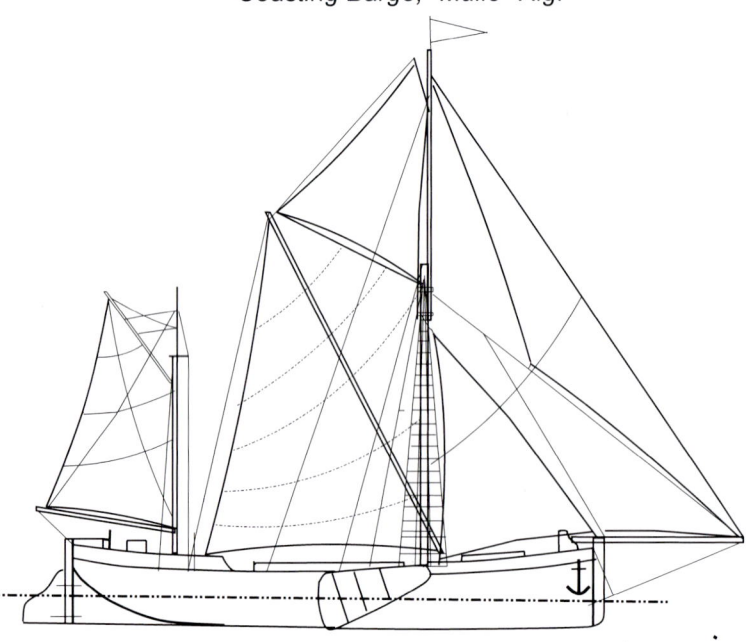

The so called "Mulie" rig, gets it's name from the combination of a spritsail rigged main mast and a ketch rigged mizzen. This gave the advantage of a large sail area without the need for a prohibitively long sprit which could prove dangerously cumbersome in open waters and high winds.

The 90 foot *Cambria* races in the same class as the 40 foot *Cygnet* ( above right). Strange bed fellows perhaps but it seems to work!

# The Racing Barge crew

Although usually only carrying a crew of two or three, the extra workload involved with racing means that the rules for barges competing in matches allow for a crew of five including the Skipper. The traditional set up is as follows-

**Aft**

*Skipper:* Who is of course in over all command of the barge and who will usually be steering.

*Mainsheetman*: Acts as "Eyes" of the Skipper and is often the tactician on board, sometimes being considered as important as the Skipper. The mainsheet man is in charge of trimming the sails, adjusting the sheets etc. Controls the mainsheet when gybing. Also raises and lowers lee boards.

*One additional crew member* : assisting with sheets and lee boards.

**Forward**

*Two crew members:* Looking after the head sails and sheets at the front. A very busy position especially on a Bowsprit barge.

Crew positions are not static and crew members move around as required this ability to work as a team is particularly significant when the barge gybes. ("changes course by swinging the sail across a following wind"- Dictionary definition. "A large heavy sail sweeps across the deck looking for an unwary head"- Lay definition).

In a racing crew everyone has their job to do and this must be done at the right time and in unison. For this reason most Barge Match committees award cups for "Seamanship".

*" A very busy position especially on a Bowsprit barge".*

## What makes a good racing Skipper?

However good the barge and however experienced the crew, if the Skipper does not have the ability to make the best use of these resources, he or she will not be consistently successful.

So what does make a successful racing Skipper? A blend of the following would seem to be a good starting point-
- Experience
- Skill
- Enthusiasm
- Competitiveness

All the above contribute to having the knack of reading weather, tide and the general situation in such a way as to get the best out of a barge in challenging and changing conditions.

A racing Skipper needs to have a good situational awareness of what is happening around and indeed under the barge. He or she must be able to manoeuvre with an awareness of other traffic to maintain safety, while anticipating the manoeuvres of the other barges in the match in an attempt to gain a tactical advantage.

A key element in sailing a racing barge is the ability to trim the barge to it's optimum by setting sails and lee boards for the greatest possible efficiency. To do this the Skipper needs to know how to adjust the sails to get the best out of them in the conditions. As an example, In very windy conditions sails need to be set as flat as possible. In low winds they need to be set to give a fuller shape to catch as much wind as possible. The set of the sails is not the only way to increase the efficiency of the sailing rig. The rake, or angle of the main mast can be altered within certain limits, this being set slightly more forward in windy conditions than it would be in calmer air.

It is not just the sails which can be adjusted to give the best possible trim. The lee boards also need to be set to optimise performance. These can be set in more than one position on most barges. Their location, further forward or aft has an effect on the over all "balance" of the barge. The more efficiently the barge is balanced, the less drag is incurred and thus and the more speed is obtained.

Although it is not necessary for a Skipper to have an intimate knowledge of all the sometimes complex rules covering Barge Matches in general and the local variations applying to the match being contested in particular, a good general knowledge of these is, of course, essential.

As with any form of competition, skill is not enough on it's own. There has also to be that enthusiasm, competitiveness and leadership which welds a crew into a unit which can achieve it's maximum racing potential.

There is more to being a good Skipper than just being able to drive a barge.

# Sails carried for racing

Most of the sails carried by the racing barges of today have been made using traditional methods handed down from generation to generation and in Sail Lofts unchanged since the barge's heyday.

All the barges currently racing carry their sails on a spritsail rig, their main sail being carried on a sprit rather than the gaff and boom arrangement common on fishing smacks. Although some of the larger barges such as *Cambria* and *Thalatta* also have a gaff and boom mizzen, this "Mulie" rig does not have a separate classification for racing.

For the purposes of the rules of racing, barges are classified in two basic classes relating to the sail plan they use.

*Staysail class.* Barges without a bowsprit or, very occasionally, one choosing to raise its bowsprit and race as a staysail barge.

Local rules may stipulate that there should be no changing of sails during a race limiting the barge to just one staysail. Barges often have a large staysail for working in light airs and a working staysail for general conditions. They may also carry a smaller one for working in strong winds. Running sails are as large and full as practicable in order to catch the maximum amount of wind.

*Bowsprit class.* Logically enough, a barge carrying and using a bowsprit. Choices of sails are largely unrestricted. Additional sails can be carried. The choice of sails is largely down to the preference and pocket depth of the owners! Running sails, as with the Staysail Class, are cut fuller and larger than those which would be serviceable for general use, these having a much flatter form.

Booms can be carried to "Boom out" main and foresails when running before the wind to catch as much of that wind as possible. This can clearly be seen in this study of *Xylonite* racing in the 2016 Thames Match.

## What makes a good Racing Barge?

Even a brief study of the Sailing Barge Association Barge Championship results over recent years will indicate that some barges are significantly more successful than others when it comes to winning races. There are a number of reasons for this, not all of them related to the physical attributes of the barges themselves.

Barge racing is not a professional sport nor is it one in which victory brings great kudos or reputation outside the sailing barge community. While some owners race their barges for the thrill and rewards of competition, others do so largely for the social side and the pleasure in having an enjoyable sail round in good company. Whatever the reason owners and crew have for taking part, many consider that the sailing barge matches provide much of the life blood which keeps these historic vessels active.

While barge racing has evolved over the years, not all the barges have enjoyed the amount of investment needed to keep up. As stated above, some owners may be highly competitive and be willing and able to spend money on keeping their vessel in top racing condition, but others are either less able or are unwilling to do so. The East Coast Sail Trust owned *Thalatta* for instance is equipped and rigged specifically for work with school aged young people and while she may occasionally take part in matches, she is unlikely to be sailed or equipped in a way to make her competitive.

To return to the question of, "what makes a good racing barge?" There are of course, a number of factors involved.

As with any other racing machine on water, land, or in the air, to be successful the greatest possible efficiency must be achieved. That is, to slightly paraphrase the true scientific definitions, the most speed must be obtained for the least effort. To this can be added the need to manoeuvre efficiently and to be able to do all these things in variable and often unpredictable conditions using only the power of the wind and tide. Put these together and you potentially have a successful racing barge.

Factors which can make a racing barge more efficient include its weight, the shape of the hull, the size of the gear the cut and rig of the sails and even such details as removing the prop to reduce drag where the barge is fitted with an engine. Since the use of engines in a race is not permitted, the absence of one becomes a distinct weight saving advantage!

Barges racing today may carry much larger gear than they did "In trade". For instance, *Reminder* when she was rigged to win the 1929 Thames barge match was equipped with huge gear, far too big for a working crew of two to manage Although this rig is no longer carried she still uses racing gear approximately ten percent bigger than she would have done as a working barge.

Today, barges which specialise in racing carry larger gear than others, while any racing barge is likely to carry one or more sails bigger than the day to day working rig of old. The crew of five permitted under race rules is well able to operate such a rig efficiently. Such a large crew would be as impractical for day to day operation today as when they were sailing commercially when two, or on some of the larger spritsail barges, three people were a sufficient crew to handle the working gear. It was this ability to be sailed by such a small crew which lead to the spritsail rig largely replacing the much more labour intensive ketch rig by the early Twentieth Century.

Part of the natural evolution of the sailing barge was the experimentation with variations on the basic hull shape by builders and owners until they arrived at one which they considered to be the most efficient for their particular needs. This is all reflected in the relative performance of the current barge fleet.

Today technology and design still plays it's part with even the humble lee board benefiting from scientific streamlining and lightening. On working barges the lee boards were usually constructed from wood and were flat with just the leading and trailing edges rounded off to reduce drag. Although the majority of barges still employ this type of board, some, particularly if used for racing, now use an aerofoil shaped board. Mounted with the convex side of the board nearest the hull these boards generate a "Lifting" force against down wind drift. Because of their shape these hydrofoil shaped lee boards also generate less drag. The lightest and most efficient of these boards are now made from metal.

A less scientific, but significant contribution to success can be gained from the arduous but worthwhile task of ensuring that the bottom of the barge has been efficiently cleaned of marine life. The resulting reduction in drag can lead to a significant increase in the efficiency of the barge.

The two barges referred to in this section. The schools ship *Thalatta* (left) and Topsail Charter's *Reminder* (right). There is a Newsreel clip of *Reminder* competing in the 1934 Thames Match at:

*www.britishpathe.com/video/video/round-the-mouse*

# Racing tactics

Success in barge racing is, in some ways as dependent on the tactical ability of the crew as on the performance of the barge itself.

From the spectators point of view, the start of a Match is often the most exciting part as barges vie for the most favourable position, fighting for what little breeze their may be on a still early morning, perhaps with very little room. In this respect the Colne and Pin Mill Matches can be the most challenging, both starting in narrow rivers.

It is at the start that the situational awareness of the Skipper and crew is tested to the limits. Barges are competing for position at close quarters, manoeuvring to either win the Trophy for being first over the line after the Start Gun, or playing a longer game, to be in a more advantageous position i.e. up to windward for the race. Sometimes both these elements combine for a good start.

In doing this the barge Skippers have to concentrate on avoiding collisions and following those race rules intended to minimise the chance of such accidents. Each Skipper will be looking to be in a position where other barges have to give way, ideally being on a Starboard tack which always has priority. If the the barges to windward are forced to give way, so much the better.

While a skipper is not necessarily expected to have an intimate knowledge of all the race rules (they can be pages long and complicated) He/She needs a working knowledge of the basics for safe and fair conduct. Rules for Barge Matches are decided by and adjudicated by the Committee of the Match being raced. There is no formal umpire or referee, with the application of the rules being considered to be "Consensual" with an implied duty of sportsmanship to compete within the rules.

Competitors have the right to raise a challenge or "Protest" arising from anything which has taken place during the race if they believe that a competing barge has breached any of the race rules. If this happens the matter will be decided by the Match Committee.

During the race an intimate knowledge of local conditions can be decisive, as small details such as the size and position of trees or buildings on the river bank can effect the strength and direction of the wind. Familiarity with the flow of the tide in the area being sailed together with the depth of water likely to be encountered can be crucial. More than one Skipper has found himself stuck on the sand at Mersea Stone at the start of a Colne Match!

The ability to read the weather is essential in order to sail a competitive race, wind speed and direction does not often remain constant. The Skipper who has his barge best trimmed to work to windward has an advantage.

Tactically it is important to sail with the longest tacks possible as every gybe or change of direction reduces speed. Staysail barges are able to sail closer to the wind than Bowsprit barges but the latter are faster which compensates for the longer tacks they have to make. It goes without saying that, as with other forms of competitive sailing, stealing the other vessels wind by getting between it and the breeze is a legitimate and effective tactic.

Two photographs illustrating the challenges of a good race start. Tacking in the early morning mist on the Colne (Top) A narrow river with plenty of other craft to avoid. A good look out is essential! (L to R) *Marjorie, Decima, Reminder, Repertor, Cygnet.* The bottom picture shows four barges (L to R) *Melissa, Niagara, Repertor* and *Edith May* charging for the start line off Southend Pier.

# The individual Barge Matches
## Medway

**Usual course;** Gillingham Pier to Medway Buoy (or alternative) and back.
**Best viewing points;** Gillingham Pier, Strand leisure park. Footpath around St. Mary's Island, Chatham. Eastern point of the Isle of Grain.
**Brief History;** Racing has taken place on the Medway since the 1870's. In 1949 the Marina Club at Hoo organised the first of 5 matches for yacht barges. Commercial craft raced again in 1954. The modern series started in 1965.
**Web Site;** www.medwaybargematch.co.uk

### Classes contested with results 2016

***Restricted Staysail Class***
Prizes awarded;

1st (Challenge Cup presented by Rochester Upon Medway Borough Council, Challenge Cup for Master - The Jim Diddams Memorial Trophy, Championship Pennant presented by Armac Shipping Services Ltd) *Niagara*

2nd (Challenge Cup presented by W M & A. Quinney Ltd) *Edith May*

3rd (Silver Jubilee Cup, presented by P Goldsmith) *Repertor*
First across the start line - (Challenge Cup presented by J P Knight) *Niagara*
First to the outer mark - (Challenge Cup presented by Lloyds) *Niagara*

***Bowsprit Class***
Prizes awarded;

. 1st (Challenge Cup in memory of Maurice Gill CBE, presented by Crescent Shipping Ltd. Challenge Cup for Master, The Jim Diddams Memorial Trophy, Championship Pennant presented by Armac Shipping Services Ltd) *Edme*

2nd (Challenge Cup presented by Tate and Lyle Ltd.) *Mirosa*

3rd *Marjorie*
First across the start line (Challenge Cup presented by Gransden Marine Ltd) *Mirosa*
First to the Outer Mark (Vic Wadhams Memorial Trophy) *Mirosa*
Seamanship Award *Pudge*

***Coasting Class***
Prizes awarded;

1st (The Coasting Class Cup, The Championship Pennant) *Cambria*

2nd *Pudge*

3rd *Lady of the Lea*
First across the start line *Lady of the Lea*
First to outer mark *Pudge*
**Date 2017** Saturday 3 June
**Date 2018** Saturday 19 May

## Note to the Medway Match history

In the forward to the 2016 Match Program, Organising Committee Chairman Geoffrey Gransdon included the following-

*"Last summer we were contacted by Mr Sydney Platt, acting on behalf of the Medway Towns Rowing Club, whom amongst their presentation prize cups, held one in particular last awarded in 1923 and again in 1924 as the Simmons Cup. The inscription on the cup reads as follows-*
*20th Annual Sailing Barge Match*
*FIRST PRIZE FOR SPRITSAIL SAILING BARGES*
*Presented by the Subscribers*
*Won By: T Simmons, June 1873!*

Taken at face value this cup would seem to throw some doubt on the generally accepted view that the first Match took place on the Thames in 1863 as related earlier in this book. However, Barge Match historian Chris Kite and others have defended the status quo robustly, citing a report in the *Chatham News and North Kent Spectator* of June 14 1873 which refers to "The first annual match" having just taken place on the Medway. It has also been pointed out that *Lloyd's Weekly Newspaper* of 8 June 1873 announced that the "First Medway Barge Match" was to start in that year.

There is a suggestion that the cup in question may in fact refer to a race on the Thames and that the Trophy had merely been in the keeping of the Medway club. Whatever the truth, some interesting questions are asked which no doubt will be pontificated on for some time yet!

## Blackwater (with Smack Race)

**Usual course;** Maldon, off Osea Island, to Wallet Spitway Buoy and return to finish off Osea Island.

**Best viewing points;** Stansgate sea wall, near Marconi Sailing Club. (Take Stansgate Rd. Off Bradwell Rd. Nb limited parking.) Also St Lawrence Bay and Bradwell though they may be farther from the action.

**Brief History;** The Match has been organised by the Blackwater Sailing Barge Match Association since 1962.

**Web Site**

### Classes contested with 2016 results

*Staysail and small barges*
Prizes awarded;

1st *Cygnet*

2nd *Blackthorn*

3rd *Pudge*

First round the outer mark *Blackthorn*
First across the start line *Cygnet*

*Senior Staysail*
Prizes awarded;

1st *Niagara*

2nd *Edith May*

First round the outer mark *Niagara*
First across the start line *Edith May*

*Bowsprit*

1st *Edme*

2nd *Mirosa*

3rd *Dawn*

First round the outer mark *Mirosa*
First across the start line *Dawn*

**Date 2017** Saturday 17 June
**Date 2018** Saturday 7 July

## Passage Match

**Usual course;** Gravesend (but see below) to the Orwell No 1 Buoy off Harwich. This gives a race distance of approximately 54 nautical miles.

**Best viewing points;** Gravesend, Southend and Walton Piers, Dovercourt.

**Brief History;** Inaugurated in 1978 by Blue Circle industries as the "Blue Circle Challenge Match" for a passage from Gravesend to the Orwell.

This Match has not been contested since 2012 though it is scheduled again for 2017 but only as a low key "feeder" event for Pin Mill. However, interest is growing in this Match again with Queenborough as a new starting point off the Isle of Sheppey. It may be that the event returns to the Sailing Barge Championship in the not too distant future.

## Classes contested
Prizes awarded;
1st
2nd
3rd
Fastest start.
Results from this race no longer qualify for the Sailing Barge Championship. When raced the Match acts as a feeder for the Pin Mill Match the following week,
**Date 2017** Saturday 24 June
**Date 2018** Saturday 16 June (Provisional)

## Pin Mill
**Usual course;** Butterman's Bay, near Pin Mill. Out and back. The Officer of the day has up to twenty possible courses to choose from depending on conditions at the start.

**Best viewing point;** River edge from Butterman's Bay Eastward. (Near "Butt and Oyster"). Shotley Marina, Harwich.

**Brief History;** Organised by the Pin Mill Sailing Club, the first race, won by *Memory*, was as part of the Regatta of 1962. *Marjorie*, still a keen race competitor, was one of these pioneering entries. In 1963 the Barge Match became a separate event in it's own right. A popular event, the Match had the greatest number of entrants in the Queen's Silver Jubilee year of 1977 when twenty six barges took part.

**Web Site** *www.pmsc.org.uk/barges*

## Classes contested with results 2016
### Class A
Prizes awarded;

1st (RHYC Challenge Cup) *Mirosa*

2nd (Hedley Farrington Challenge Cup) *Marjorie*

3rd (Orvis Challenge Cup)
First round the outer mark *Mirosa*
First across start line *Marjorie*

### Class B
Prizes awarded;

1st ( PMSC Challenge Cup) *Niagara*

2nd ( Capt. Smy Challenge Cup) *Melissa*

3rd (Capt. Clark (Diberry) Challenge Cup) *Reminder*
First round the outer mark *Niagara*
First across start line *Melissa*

### Class C
Prizes awarded;

1st (Henry Filmer Challenge Cup) *Adieu*

2nd (Cavendish Moton Challenge Cup) *Ardwina*

3rd (Tolly Cobold Challenge Cup) *Pudge*
First round the outer mark *Adieu*
First across start line *Blackthorn*
Overall Champion (J Lawrence Winner's Pennant) *Niagara*
Seamanship Award (Harold Smy Memorial Cup)
Award for Merit (Mick Lungley Memorial)
Overall excellence (Bill Hatley Memorial)
Spiro Ling Trophy for the fastest start overall *Melissa*
**Date 2017**   Saturday 1 July
**Date 2018**   Saturday 23 June

### Thames

**Usual course;** Start at Mucking No. 3 buoy, out to the South West Barrow Buoy and back to a finish at Gravesend, subject to weather conditions.

**Brief History;** Founded by Henry Dodd in 1863. After a lapse of a number of years, the Match was revived by Captain Mark Boyle to commemorate the fiftieth anniversary of VE Day in 1995. Such was Mark Boyle's influence in it's continued revival that following his sudden death in 2012, the One Hundred and Fiftieth anniversary Match the following year was named in his honour.

The Match is claimed to be "The second oldest organised sailing race after the America's Cup" and "The longest running, regularly organised, National racing event for traditional sail in the world".

**Best viewing point;** Anchor Cove, off Royal Pier Rd, Gravesend.

**Web Site**   *www.thamesmatch.co.uk*

### Classes contested with results 2016

**Champion Bowsprit Class**

Prizes awarded;

1st *Edme*

2nd *Adieu*

3rd *Xylonite*

**Champion Staysail Class**

Prizes awarded;

1st *Niagara*

2nd *Edith May*

**Coasting Class**

Prizes awarded;

1st *Cambria*

2nd *Lady of the Lea*

Prizes awarded;(Over all Match)
Master making the Fastest Start: Geoff Gransden, *Edith May*
Master of the Fastest Barge to the Mark: Peter Sands, *Niagara*
Master of the Fastest Barge over the Course: Andy Harman, *Edme*
Best Seamanship in the Match: Richard Titchner, *Xylonite*
Best Seamanship at the outer mark: Andy Harman, *Edme*

Best Seamanship at the Start: Geoff Gransden, *Edith May*
Best performing Mainsheetman: Cyril Varley, *Cambria*
Most valued crew member: Deben Johnson, *Cambria*
For achievement of a young crew member: Harley Deards, *Niagara*
**Date 2017**  Saturday 15 July
**Date 2018**  Saturday 21 July

## Swale (with Smack Race)

**Usual course;**  Start line off Sand End Buoy in the east Swale, out to marks in the estuary and return to finish off Faversham Creek.

**Best viewing point**   Sheppey shore, Harty Ferry, Shellness, Leysdown, Seasalter Shore, Sportsman foreshore, Tankerton Slopes, Herne Bay.

**Brief History;** Matches are organised by the Kentish Sail Association which was founded in the delightful Shipwrights Arms in the early 1970s. The first match on the Swale took place on 21 September 1973 (The KSA. Had organised one on the Thames in June as part of the Greenwich festival).

This first Match was contested by *Mirosa, Pudge, Olive May, Montreal, Ironsides, Ethal Maud and Alice May*. Victory went to *Mirosa* with Jimmy Diddams as Skipper. Other barges were in attendance, *Cabby* as Committee boat and *Seagul II* and *Xylonite* following. The Steamer *Puffin* and some gaffers and smacks were also present.

A unique feature of this first Match was that the barges started at anchor with sails brailed. This was not reported to have been universally popular and is not a feature of today's Matches.

### Classes contested

**Class 3 Bowsprit**
Prizes awarded;

1st (CTS Cup) *Edme*

2nd (Swale Trophy) *Marjorie*

3rd (Crescent Cup)
Fastest start: *Edme*

**Class 4 Staysail**
Prizes awarded;

1st (Hurliman Cup) *Edith May*

2nd ( Kay Allen Cup) *Niagara*

3rd ( Percy Wildish Cup) *Repertor*
Fastest start: *Edith May*

**Class 5 Restricted Staysail**
Prizes awarded;

1st (Brent Cup) *Lady of the Lea*

2nd ( Morgan-le-Faye Cup) *Orinoco*

3rd *Centaur*
Fastest start Class 5: *Lady of the Lea*

Fastest elapsed time Classes 3/4/5
Last barge timed home (Don Grover Memorial Trophy)
Seamanship in Classes 3/4/5 *Niagara*
**Date 2017**   Saturday 29 July
**Date 2018**   Saturday 4 August

## Southend

**Usual course;** Start and finish from marker buoy at the end of Southend Pier. Course, depending on conditions, is usually a figure of eight, East and West of the Pier.

**Best viewing point;** Southend Pier. Superb view looking down on the barges, particularly at the start.

**Brief History;** Originally part of Southend's Regatta. The Match was revived in 1964 as part of the Golden Jubilee Celebrations. Supported by Southend Corporation, the Match is usually well supported by events and commentary at the Pier head.

**Web Site** *www.thamesbarge.org.uk/southendbargematch*

### Classes contested

**Class A Bowsprit**
Prizes awarded;

1st *Xylonite*

2nd *Marjorie*

3rd *Adieu*

**Class B  Champion Staysail**
Prizes awarded;

1st *Niagara*

2nd *Melissa*

**Class C Staysail**

1st *Lady of the Lea*

2nd *Defiance*

First round the outer mark overall: *Niagara*
Fastest start overall: *Xylonite*
Seamanship: *Xylonite*
**Date 2017**   Sunday 27 August
**Date 2018**   Sunday 26 August

## Colne (with Smack Race)

**Usual course;** From Batemans Tower, Brightlingsea to Colne Point With a mark off Clacton Pier.

**Best viewing point;** Mersea Stone. Bateman's Tower, Brightlingsea

**Brief History;** The Colne Smack Race was first organised in 1971 by the *Colne Smack Preservation Society*. The Barge Match was introduced the next year.

## Classes contested

All barges taking part usually race as though in a single class with only one award for the fastest start and no award for the first barge round the outer mark
Prizes awarded;

1st (TSB Cup) *Edme*

2nd (Sailorman Cup) *Niagara*

3rd (Prior Cup) *Repertor*

Golden Cockerel award for the "First barge over the start line" *Edme*
Seamanship Award, Smacks and Barges

Barges sail in a single class for this event but are judged as if sailing in 3 classes as defined in the current Championship points system. There is only one award (2 points) for first across the start line, and no awards for first round the outer mark in this race

**Date 2017** Saturday 2nd September

**Date 2018** Saturday 1st September

## Whitstable Harbour Day

Although not included in the sailing barge championship, racing for traditional sailing craft takes place at the Whitstable Harbour Regatta each August The usual course for traditional craft has the Start/finish line between East Quay Pier head and Oyster buoy.

As well as a good day out, the event gives the opportunity to see such delightful vessels as traditional Oyster Smacks & Bawleys, replica Smacks & Bawleys, other traditional gaff rigged craft and of course Thames Sailing Barges.

**Web site** *www.whitstableharbour.org*

Prizes awarded;

1st

2nd

3rd

**Date 2017** Saturday 5 August

# The Racing Barges

Those barges which are most likely to be seen competing in Barge Matches in the second decade of the Twenty First Century are listed in the following pages. Each is illustrated with a full page photograph and has a short narrative giving an insight into it's history. Results achieved in Barge Matches for the three years to January 2017 have been given for each barge. These act both as a guide to competitiveness and as an indication of which Matches owners choose to contest. Please note however that past attendance does not guarantee future appearances!

To help spectators recognise each barge, a heading "Aids to identification" has been included, listing such relevant information as the colour of the Bob, sprit and hull. (Where a hull colour is not mentioned it can be assumed to be black). Distinctive features such as logos and motifs visible in sails are also included, though please note, as with other identification features these can be changed at the owners discretion.

Barges are shown in alphabetical order within the Classes they contest in the Sailing Barge Association organised Sailing Barge Championship. The barges in each class are as follows-

## Bowsprit Class

*Adieu     Marjorie*
*Cabby     Mirosa*
*Dawn      Xylonite*
*Edme*

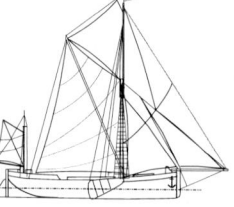

## Fast Staysail Class

*Ardwina    Niagara*
*Edith May  Reminder*
*Greta      Repertor*
*Melissa*

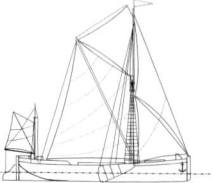

## Slow Staysail /Coasting Class

*Blackthorn  Lady Daphne*
*Cambria     Lady of the Lea*
*Centaur     Orinoco*
*Cygnet      Pudge*
*Defiance    Thalatta*
*Dinah*

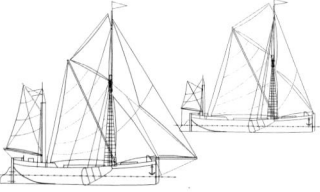

Placings given in the results section refer to finishing positions in the barges Class rather than in the over finishing position except where indicated.

## Relative sizes of the barges

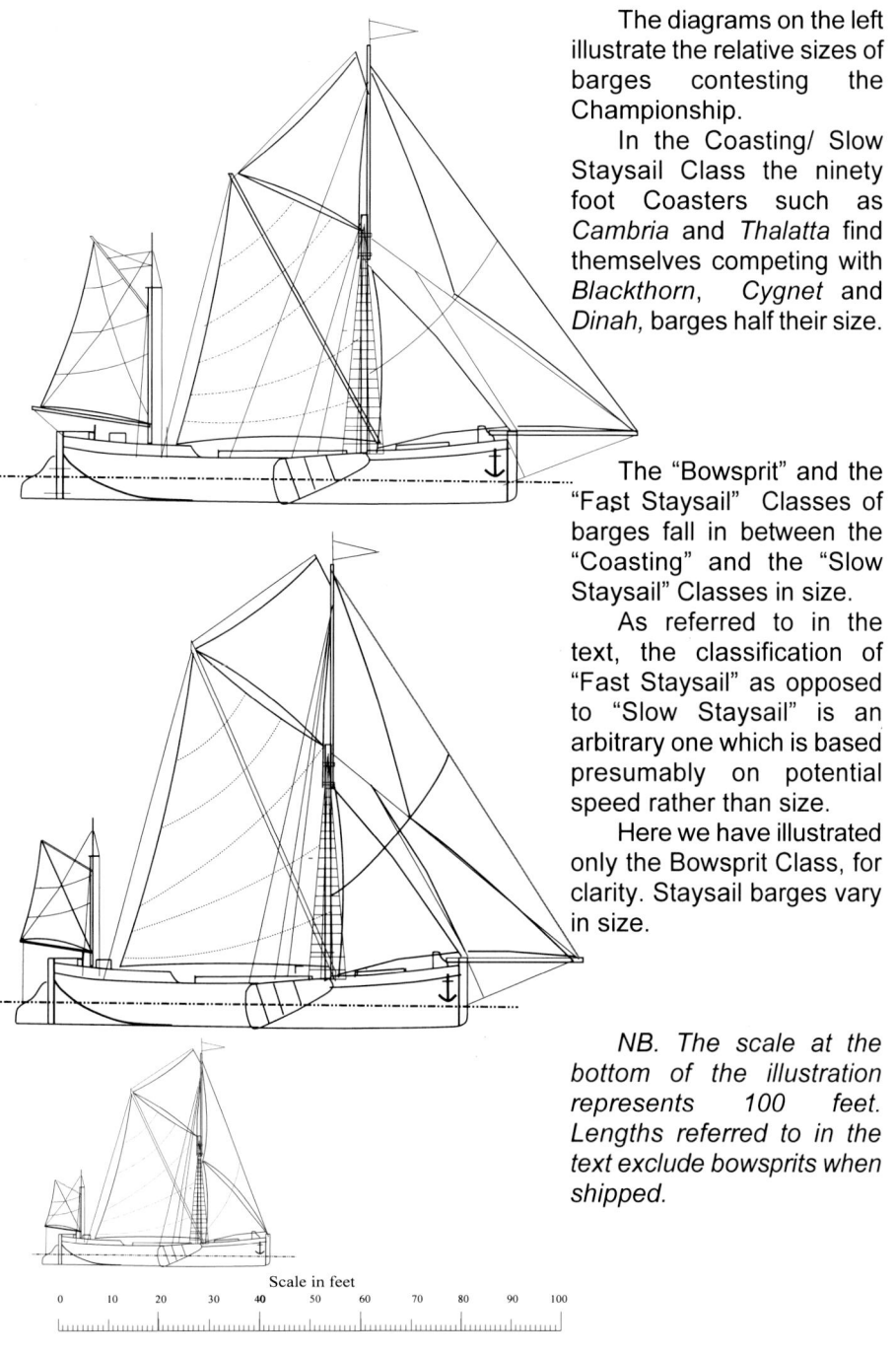

The diagrams on the left illustrate the relative sizes of barges contesting the Championship.

In the Coasting/ Slow Staysail Class the ninety foot Coasters such as *Cambria* and *Thalatta* find themselves competing with *Blackthorn*, *Cygnet* and *Dinah,* barges half their size.

The "Bowsprit" and the "Fast Staysail" Classes of barges fall in between the "Coasting" and the "Slow Staysail" Classes in size.

As referred to in the text, the classification of "Fast Staysail" as opposed to "Slow Staysail" is an arbitrary one which is based presumably on potential speed rather than size.

Here we have illustrated only the Bowsprit Class, for clarity. Staysail barges vary in size.

NB. *The scale at the bottom of the illustration represents 100 feet. Lengths referred to in the text exclude bowsprits when shipped.*

Scale in feet
0  10  20  30  **40**  50  60  70  80  90  100

# ADIEU

## ADIEU of Harwich
*Official No. 161035*

**Bowsprit Class**

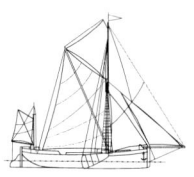

**Construction** - Steel
**Dimensions** - Length 87.9 ft Beam 19.4 ft
**Bob** - Plain light blue
**Bowsprit** - Yes
**Mizzen** - Small
**Davits** - At stern
**Other recognition features**- Black sprit with thin white band.
**Notes** - *Adieu* was built as a 79 ton spritsail barge in 1929 by Horlock's of Mistley for F W Horlock & Co Ltd, a sister ship to *Portlight, Xylonite, Reminder, Repertor and Resourceful.* All of which remain with us today. *Blue Mermaid,* the other barge built at this yard is not, though a reproduction is under construction for the Sea Change Sailing Trust.

*Adieu* served with Horlock's for most of her trading life, being converted to a motor barge in 1949 and laid up as a lighter in 1967. She was saved from dereliction by James Stewart in 1985.

Following long term restoration she is now a barge yacht owned and Skippered by Iolo Brooks and based at St. Katharine's Dock.

**Matches entered 2016**
Medway 4th, Thames 2nd, Pin Mill 1st, Southend 3rd
**Position in Class**
Fifth
**Over all Championship position**
Eighth

**Matches entered 2015**
Medway 2nd, Thames 1st, Southend 1st
**Position in Class**
Third
**Over all Championship position**
Fifth

**Matches entered 2014**
Medway 3rd, Blackwater 2nd, Southend 1st, also First round outer mark and fastest start in class
**Over all Championship position**
Fifth

**CABBY** *Dunkirk Little Ship*

## CABBY of Rochester
### Bowsprit Class
*Official No. 160687*

**Construction** - Wood
**Dimensions** - Length 91.93 ft Beam 21.5 ft
**Bob** - Plain white C on plain red ground
**Bowsprit** - Yes
**Mizzen** - Small
**Davits** - At stern
**Other recognition features** - Dark grey lower hull with black wale. Plain brown sprit.

**Notes** - The last full size barge built of wood at Rochester, *Cabby* was constructed by Gill for the London & Rochester Barge Company. Work started in 1925 but because of the economic climate, she was not completed until three years later.

In 1940, when at Ipswich, she was ordered to Dunkirk with drums of freshwater for the troops. Redirected to Brest, she was finally ordered to Plymouth without reaching France! Subsequent war service saw her visit Ireland, the Clyde and the Hebrides where she was given a new wheelhouse.

After the war, as a motor barge, *Cabby* carried cargoes such as cement, china clay and Portland stone travelling as far afield as Antwerp. Finishing cargo work in the late 1960's, *Cabby* worked on as a passenger carrier before being re-rigged in 1970 and used as a company charter barge.

*Cabby* has had several subsequent owners, including Sailing Barge Cabby Ltd who operated her as a charter barge on the River Thames. She displayed this companies logo on her mizzen sail when she competed in the Blackwater (pictured) and Swale Matches in 2013.

Having changed hands, *Cabby* had her stem replaced, and decks repaired In the Summer of 2015, following which her new owner stated his intention of recommencing racing "If a sail sponsor can be found to assist with the cost of servicing the rigging, dressing the sails and general servicing work to preparing her for sailing".

Although not having returned to competition in 2016 there remains the possibility that *Cabby* will do so in the future.

**Web site** - *www.sbcabby.wordpress.com*

**Matches entered 2016**
None

**Matches entered 2015**
None

**Matches entered 2014**
None

**DAWN** *Dunkirk Little Ship*

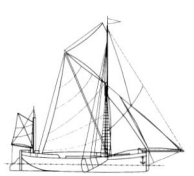

## DAWN of Maldon
*Official No. 105902*

**Bowsprit Class**

**Construction** - Wood
**Dimensions** - Length 81.9 ft Beam 20 ft
**Bob** - Plain blue
**Bowsprit** - Yes
**Mizzen** - Small
**Davits** - At stern
**Other recognition features** - Cream trim to gunwale. Grey hull. Cream sprit. Tiller steered.

**Notes** - *Dawn* was built by Walter Cook of Maldon in 1897 as a 54 ton spritsail "Stackie" barge intended for the carriage of hay and straw.

*Dawn* was part of "Operation Dynamo" the evacuation of Allied troops from France in 1940 and is listed as a "Dunkirk Little Ship" despite being damaged before reaching the French coast and having to return to Maldon for repairs.

Becoming a motor barge, then a lighter, *Dawn* was rescued by Gordon Swift, in 1967, re-rigged and used as a charter barge from Maldon. 1978 saw her with the Passmore Edwards Museum of Newham who used her for children's trips.

A period of disuse and general deterioration followed until she was rescued by the formation of the "Dawn Sailing Barge Trust" which, with the help of the Heritage Lottery Fund completed her restoration at Heybridge in 2008.

In 2014 work was carried out at the St. Osyth Boat Yard to restore *Dawn* to her original tiller steered configuration.

Now regularly Skippered by Gerrard Swift *Dawn* is currently based at Maldon and available for charter work.

**Web site** - *www.dawn1897.com*

**Matches entered 2016**
Blackwater 3rd and "Fastest start"
**Position in Class**
Eighth
**Over all Championship position**
Equal seventeenth

**Matches entered 2015**
None
**Position in Class**
N/A
**Over all Championship position**
N/A

**Matches entered 2014**
None
**Over all Championship position**
N/A

# EDME

## EDME of Harwich — Bowsprit Class
*Official No. 105425*

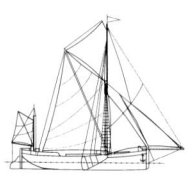

**Construction** - Wood
**Dimensions** - Length 80 ft Beam 17.25 ft
**Bob** - White 'H' on red ground
**Bowsprit** - Yes
**Mizzen** - Small
**Davits** - At stern
**Other recognition features** - White 'EDME' in topsail. Plain cream sprit.

**Notes** - *Edme* was built by J & H Cann at Harwich in 1898 for F W Horlock. Named after the English Diastatic Malt Extract Company *Edme* continued in trade under sail until 1949 when she was de-rigged and used as a lighter by Brown and Co. Subsequently, *Edme* underwent restoration at Maldon before being bought by the Harman-Harrison Consortium in 1989.

Further restoration was carried out at Skipper Andy Harman's boat yard at St.Osyth, in 2013/14 with the aid of a subsidy from the National Historic Ships Register. Based at the St Osyth Boat Yard *Edme* works as a static and cruising charter barge.

*Edme* is one of the few barges never to have been fitted with an engine which together with her high standard of maintenance helps to account for her remarkable speed and consistently good racing record.

**Web site** - *www.edmebarge.com*

### Matches entered 2016
Medway 1st, Blackwater 1st, Thames 1st, Skipper Andy Harman also received awards for "Best Seamanship at the outer mark" and "Master of the fastest barge overall", Swale 1st and "Fastest start for barge in class", Colne 1st

**Position in Class**
First

**Over all Championship position**
Second

### Matches entered 2015
Medway 1st, Pin Mill 1st and Spiro Lang Trophy for fastest start overall, Swale 1st and "Fastest start in class"

**Position in Class**
First

**Over all Championship position**
Third

### Matches entered 2014
Medway 1st, Blackwater 1st, "Fastest start" and "First round outer mark", Pin Mill 1st, Swale 1st and "Fastest start in class", Colne 1st

**Over all Championship position**
First

# MARJORIE

## MARJORIE of Ipswich
*Official No. 113753*

**Bowsprit Class**

**Construction** - Wood
**Dimensions** - Length 84 ft Beam 19.3 ft
**Bob** - Lemon & black quarters with lemon 'D' & '105' on black quarters
**Bowsprit** - Yes
**Mizzen** - Small
**Davits** - At stern
**Other recognition features** - Sprit brown with black and yellow banding. Dark grey hull, Brown transom.
**Notes** - Built in 1902 by Orvis in Ipswich for R & W Paul Ltd and registered as a 56 ton spritsail barge. Little is known of *Marjorie's* time "In trade" except that she worked for the same owner until 1961. She was then bought by A J O'Shea, converted to a charter barge and based at Maldon.

*Marjorie* subsequently went to Albert Groom for a while before being bought by her present owner, barrister Simon Devonshire in 1993. Simon had her restored as a barge yacht by Robert Deards at Hoo in Kent. Robert together with her owner are now *Marjorie's* regular racing Skippers.

*Marjorie* is based at Robert Deard's yard at Hoo and at St Katherine's Dock in London. The winter of 2016/7 saw her undergo substantial refurbishment in preparation for the new season.

**Matches entered 2016**
Medway 3rd, Thames 4th, Pin Mill 2nd, Swale 2nd, Southend 2nd
**Position in Class**
Second
**Over all Championship position**
Fifth

**Matches entered 2015**
Medway 3rd, Swale 2nd, Southend 2nd and "Fastest start overall", Colne 2nd
**Position in Class**
Second
**Over all Championship position**
Fourth

**Matches entered 2014**
Pin Mill 4th, Swale 2nd, Southend 2nd, Colne 2nd
**Over all Championship position**
Equal sixth

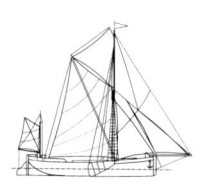

**MIROSA**

## MIROSA of Maldon
*Official No. 96488*

**Bowsprit Class**

**Construction** - Wood
**Dimensions** - Length 82 ft. Beam 20.75 ft
**Bob** - Lemon Tudor rose on blue ground
**Bowsprit** - Yes
**Mizzen** - Small
**Davits** - At stern
**Other recognition features** - Sprit cream with a black band.
**Notes** - *Mirosa* was built as the 49 ton spritsail rigged stack barge *Ready* at Maldon in 1892 by John Howard, for Charles Gutteridge of Vauxhall. Passing through the hands of Walter Keeble of Maldon and Charles Pudney, also of Maldon, *Ready* came to Francis and Gilder in 1938.

Francis and Gilder sold the name *"Ready"* to Trinity House for £35 in 1947 the barge being renamed *Mirosa*. She continued in trade until 1955 when she was used as a timber lighter by Browns of Maldon.

In 1964 *Mirosa* was purchased by Clarence Deval who had her restored with a full set of traditional flax sails, manila running rigging and wooden masts.

*Mirosa* had at least two more owners before Peter Dodds bought her in 1976. *Mirosa* is based at Iron Wharf, Favesham where she is used for charter work and racing. One of the last barges to earn her living under sail alone, *Mirosa* has never had an engine fitted,
**Contact** - 07831 328382

**Matches entered 2016**
Medway 2nd also "First across start line", "First to outer mark", Blackwater 2nd and "First round the outer mark" and "Best round the outer mark", Pin Mill 1st
**Position in Class**
Third
**Over all Championship position**
Sixth

**Matches entered 2015**
Pin Mill 2nd
**Position in Class**
Fourth
**Over all Championship position**
Seventeenth

**Matches entered 2014**
Medway 2nd, Pin Mill 2nd also "Seamanship award"
**Over all Championship position**
Ninth

# XYLONITE

**XYLONITE of Harwich**　　**Bowsprit Class**
*Official No. 145408*

**Construction** - Steel
**Dimensions** - Length 86.95 ft. Beam 18.49 ft
**Bob** - White stars & tree emblem on dark blue ground
**Bowsprit** - Yes
**Mizzen** - Small
**Davits** - At stern
**Other recognition features** - 'Avocet' emblem & Suffolk Life can faintly be seen in topsail. Sprit grey with red bands, hull light grey.
**Notes** - *Xylonite* was built at Mistley in 1926 by F W Horlock, for Horlock's barge fleet. She carried acid for plastic manufacture from London to Brantham on the River Stour and general cargo between London, Ipswich and Mistley. Sold in 1958 to Greenhythe Lighterage, *Xylonite* served as a motor barge before being re-rigged in the 1970's by Tim Eliff.

Owned and operated by the Cirdan Trust from 1985, *Xylonite* worked as a charter and sail training barge. Sold in 2007, *Xylonite* spent time at Maylandsea having work carried out before making a return to sailing in 2010.

Ownership passed to Photographer Tim Kent in the Spring of 2011, since which time *Xylonite* has undergone a considerable amount of restoration work, at Maylandsea, Faversham and at Heybridge Lock. Now a charter barge, *Xylonite* is usually based at Maldon.
**Web site** - *www.xylonite.co.uk*

**Matches entered 2016**
Thames 3rd    Skipper, Richard Titchener also won the award for "Best Seamanship", Pin Mill - Disqualified for using engine after 5 minute gun, Southend 1st Also "Fastest start and "Seamanship" awards, Colne 4th
**Position in Class**
Fourth
**Over all Championship position**
Seventh

**Matches entered 2015**
*Xylonite* was undergoing further restoration/maintenance during the Summer of 2015 and did not compete in any Matches.

**Matches entered 2014**
Colne
**Over all Championship position**
Equal eighteenth

# ARDWINA

## ARDWINA of London     Fast Staysail Class
*Official No. 129016*

**Construction** - Wood
**Dimensions** - Length 85 ft Beam 21.1 ft
**Bob** - Red 'A' & navigational dividers on 3 blue horizontal bands on white ground
**Bowsprit** - No
**Mizzen** - Small
**Davits** - At stern
**Other recognition features** - Has "Rolfe Judd" in topsail. Plain brown sprit.
**Notes** - Built by Orvis and Fuller at Ipswich, *Ardwina* was launched in 1909. She was owned by Goldsmith's of London until 1938, when, having lost her mast, she was abandoned at sea, being recovered after three days. She passed to Metcalf Motor Coasters and on to Daniels Bros.

*Ardwina* has had several owners since coming out of trade in 1959, including use as a houseboat. Since 1980 she has been operated as a charter and hospitality barge for Rolfe Judd and Co, a firm of London Architects.

*Ardwina* had a major refit at David Patient's yard at Maldon in 1989/90, her standing rigging was serviced in the winter of 2012/3 by Jim Dines and his team at Maldon. The team who re-rigged the *Cutty Sark*.

In the Winter of 2015/6 *Ardwina* underwent further refurbishment work at Rick Cardy's Maylandsea boat yard.
**Web Site** - *www.ardwina.co.uk*

**Matches entered 2016**
Pin Mill 2nd
**Position in Class**
Sixth
**Over all Championship position**
Equal seventeenth

**Matches entered 2015**
Pin Mill 1st also "First across the start line" and "First to the outer mark"
**Position in Class**
Fifth
**Over all Championship position**
Equal thirteenth

**Matches entered 2014**
Pin Mill 2nd
**Over all Championship position**
Equal fifteenth

# EDITH MAY

**EDITH MAY of Harwich**     **Fast Staysail Class**
*Official No.116180*

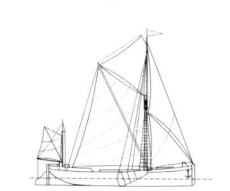

**Construction** - Wood
**Dimensions** - Length 86 ft Beam 20.75 ft
**Bob** - light blue, with a dark blue circle containing a wheat sheaf
**Bowsprit** - No
**Mizzen** - Small
**Davits** - At stern
**Other recognition features** - Cream sprit with blue band. Dark grey hull with gold/white trim.
**Notes** - *Edith May* was built as a spritsail barge by J & H Cann of Harwich in 1906 for Wm. J Barrette to carry grain, though she also carried cargoes of ammunition from Felixstowe to Norfolk. She passed to Alfred Sully of London in the 1930's. After WW 2, *Edith May* was converted to a motor barge. In 1961 she was re-rigged and became a successful racing barge.

In 1999, *Edith May* was bought in a dilapidated condition and moved to Lower Halstow where a full restoration was carried out concluding with her re-launch on June 18 2010. *Edith May* works as a charter barge during the summer months,and as a Tea Room during the winter.

Bookings are taken to sail on board *Edith May* during some races.
**Web site** - *www.edithmaybargecharter.co.uk*

**Matches entered 2016**
Medway 2nd, Blackwater 2nd Also "Seamanship" award, Thames 2nd Her Master, Geoff Gransden, also received the "Master making the fastest start" and "Best seamanship at the start" awards, Pin Mill, Retired, Swale 1st Also "Fastest start in class"
**Position in Class**
Second
**Over all Championship position**
Third

**Matches entered 2015**
Medway 2nd, Pin Mill 5th Also "First across start line" and "Award of merit", Swale 1st, Thames 3rd Also "Seamanship prize"
**Position in Class**
Second
**Over all Championship position**
Second

**Matches entered 2014**
Medway 1st, Blackwater 2nd, Pin Mill 2nd Also "Award of merit", Swale 2nd, Southend 1st, Colne 2nd
**Over all Championship position**
Equal second

**GRETA** *Dunkirk Little Ship*

*Photo courtesy Steve Norris*

## GRETA of Colchester — Fast Staysail Class
*Official No. 9832*

**Construction** - Wood
**Dimensions** - Length 80 ft. Beam 20 ft
**Bob** - Red N on black & gold ground
**Bowsprit** - No
**Mizzen** - Small
**Davits** - At stern
**Other recognition features** - Topsail has white Shepherds crook and mainsail has white 'SHEPHERD NEAME, BREWER, FAVERSHAM. Sprit cream with Light Blue band trimmed with Dark blue

**Notes** - *Greta* was built by Stone of Brightlingsea in 1892 for Edward Hibbs of Brightlingsea, who ran a fleet of barges (including *Centaur* at one time) supplying the mills processing linseed oil in Colchester. From Hibbs, *Greta* passed to the fleet of Owen Parry, where she carried cargoes of grain and malt. A notable exception was when she carried the spars for the Kaiser's racing schooner!

*Greta* was sold to the London Rochester Barge Company in 1918. Passing out of trade in the 1960's, *Greta* was converted to a houseboat and re-rigged, having become a motor barge in 1951. She is currently home to her Skipper/owner Steve Norris.

2009 *Greta* carried a cargo once more when she delivered a cargo of Shepherd and Neame's beer to St Katharine's Dock for the London Festival, the barrels being unloaded in the traditional manner, using her sprit as a derrick.

As a *Dunkirk Little Ship*, *Greta* took part in the Sixtieth anniversary celebrations, in 2000, with Prince Charles spending some time on board. In May 2015 she paid a return visit to Dunkirk Harbour, sailing from Ramsgate to commemorate the Seventy Fifth anniversary of Operation Dynamo.

*Greta* has a consistently busy schedule sailing from her Whitstable base so has not been able to compete in any of the Championship barge Matches recently. She does however regularly take part in the Whitstable Harbour event which sees a number of historic craft including barges and smacks competing in a fairly relaxed atmosphere.

We have included *Greta* in this section as it is quite possible that future bookings could involve attending Matches either as a competitor or spectator.

**Web site** - *www.greta1892.co.uk*

**Matches entered 2016**
None

**Matches entered 2015**
None

**Matches entered 2014**
None

# MELISSA

## MELISSA of London     Fast Staysail Class
*Official No. 110078*

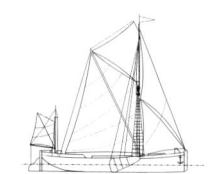

**Construction** - Steel
**Dimensions** - Length 85.3 ft. Beam 19.2 ft
**Bob** - Red and white horizontal stripes
**Bowsprit** - No
**Mizzen** - Small
**Davits** - At stern
**Other recognition features** - Cream sprit, Red hull and black lee boards.
**Notes** - Built by J G Fay of Southampton in 1899, *Melissa* was one of twenty eight built by them for E J and W Goldsmith. *Melissa* spent most of her early life carrying building materials between the South Coast and London.

In 1942 *Melissa* was bought by LRTC, two years later she was de-rigged and re-registered as a motor barge with a Bergius diesel engine. She also had a wheelhouse fitted at this time. Sold again in 1951, *Melissa* had several owners before being sold of as a houseboat in 1975.

Deterioration followed until Jonathan Webb and his father Fred rescued her in 1994 and set about a complete restoration at Pin Mill. Returned to sailing in 2009, *Melissa* won the Pin Mill Match in her first competitive sail.

Operating as a charter barge from Pin Mill and Ipswich, her bright red hull makes *Melissa* one of the most easily recognised of the current racing barges.
**Web site** - *www.sbmelissa.co.uk*

**Matches entered 2016**
Blackwater Unplaced, Pin Mill 2nd, Also Spiro Lang Trophy for fastest start over all, Southend 2nd
**Position in Class**
Equal third
**Over all Championship position**
Equal eleventh

**Matches entered 2015**
Pin Mill 4th Also "First across the start line", Southend 3rd
**Position in Class**
Sixth
**Over all Championship position**
Equal fifteenth

**Matches entered 2014**
Blackwater Unplaced, Pin Mill, Disqualified, Southend, Retired
**Over all Championship position**
Equal fifteenth

# NIAGARA

## NIAGARA of London
*Official No. 108373*

**Fast Staysail Class**

**Construction** - Steel
**Dimensions** - Length 86 ft Beam 20 ft
**Bob** - Red with a yellow star and 5 bar gate
**Bowsprit** - No
**Mizzen** - Small
**Davits** - At stern
**Other recognition features** - Plain sprit, White hull and lee boards, the latter having black scallop trimming. Usually has "Whitton Marine" logo in Tops'l.
**Notes** - *Niagara* was built by Forrestt at Wivenhoe in 1898, as a 79 ton spritsail barge. The Tilbury Contracting & Dredging Co. Operated her in 1914 as listed in the Merchant Navy List. *Niagara* later moved to the London and Rochester Trading Company being recorded in their service in 1934 and 1938 by which time she had an auxiliary engine fitted.

*Niagara's* career very nearly ended at Deptford Creek some years ago when present owner Peter Sands was one of those asked to quote a price for cutting her up for scrap. Fortunately, it was decided that she was in far too good a condition for that! Hundreds of man hours have since passed, resulting in an attractive and highly successful racing barge.

**Matches entered 2016**
Medway 1st, Blackwater 1st, Thames 1st Also, "Master of the fastest barge to the outer mark"- Peter Sands, Pin Mill 1st, Swale 2nd Also "Seamanship" award, Southend 1st Also "First barge round the outer mark", Colne 2nd
**Position in Class**
First
**Over all Championship position**
First

**Matches entered 2015**
Medway 1st, Blackwater 1st, Thames 1st Also, "Master of the fastest barge to the outer mark"- Robert Deards, Pin Mill, Retired, Swale 2nd Also "Seamanship" award, Southend 1st Also "First barge round the outer mark", Colne 2nd
**Position in Class**
First
**Over all Championship position**
First

**Matches entered 2014**
Medway 2nd, Blackwater 1st Also "First round the outer mark", Pin Mill - Disqualified, Swale 1st, Southend 2nd, Colne 2nd
**Over all Championship position**
Equal second

# REMINDER

## REMINDER of Harwich — Fast Staysail Class
*Official No. 161033*

**Construction** - Steel
**Dimensions** - Length 87.83 ft  Beam 19.38 ft
**Bob** - Green, red & white
**Bowsprit** - No
**Mizzen** - Small
**Davits** - At stern
**Other recognition features** - Plain cream sprit, white hull, black lee boards. (Easily confused with the similarly coloured *Niagara*, *Reminder* has all black lee boards and no logo in her Tops'l).

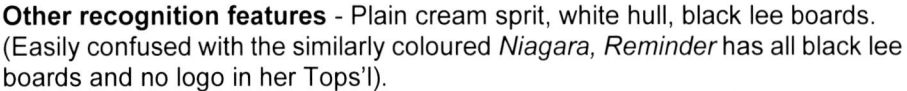

**Notes** - Built at Mistley in 1929 by Horlock's for Fred Horlock. it is said that *Reminder* was named from a promise made by Fred after the 1928 Thames Barge Match, that he would "Remind" his rivals of the speed of his barges.

*Reminder* spent much of her working life transporting acid from London to the British Xylonite Plastics Ltd factory at Manningtree, in addition to the family trade of carrying grain. Horlock's were bought by Amey Roadstone who used *Reminder* for carrying ballast. She Later passed to Webb's of Pin Mill.

In 1975 *Reminder* was sold to Roger Becket who re-rigged her and used her as a charter barge. Topsail Charters took over the barge in 2002 and operate her under the ownership of Reminder (1929) Ltd. *Reminder* is based at Maldon where she is a familiar sight operating as a busy charter barge. Her race entries are sometimes limited by her busy schedule!

**Web site** - *www.top-sail.co.uk*

**Matches entered 2016**
Blackwater, Unplaced, Pin Mill 3rd, Colne 3rd
**Position in Class**
Fifth
**Over all Championship position**
Fourteenth

**Matches entered 2015**
Pin Mill 3rd Also "Overall excellence" award, Thames 2nd Also "Master of fastest barge to the mark" award - Richard Titchener, Southend 2nd, Colne 3rd
**Position in Class**
Third
**Over all Championship position**
Sixth

**Matches entered 2014**
Blackwater, Unplaced, "Fastest start in class", Pin Mill ,Retired, Southend 4th Also "Fastest start in class", Colne, Retired
**Over all Championship position**
Eleventh

# REPERTOR

## REPERTOR of Harwich     Fast Staysail Class
*Official No. 145404*

**Construction** - Steel
**Dimensions** - Length 86 ft Beam 18.5 ft
**Bob** - White fish (Pollock) emblem with black 'P' on red ground
**Bowsprit** - No
**Mizzen** - Small
**Davits** - At stern
**Other recognition features** - Cream sprit with red band trimmed with green. Prominent red gunwale and hull below the waterline.
**Notes** - *Repertor,* meaning discoverer, explorer, inventor, innovator or deviser, was built by the boat building division of Horlock's. She was launched at Mistley in 1924 as a 69 ton spritsail barge for F.W. Horlock Ocean Transport Company.

*Repertor* was a pure sailing barge until the 1930s when she had her first auxiliary engine fitted. Later she became a motor tanker barge, for which role she had all her gear and deck removed and steel tanks installed. *Repertor* was eventually sold out of trade served for a time as a houseboat at Battersea.

Re-rigged by C McLaren in 1978 *Repertor* is now owned by David and Elaine Pollock who operate her as a charter barge. Usually based at St Katharine's Docks, at Whitstable and at Faversham. *Repertor* also operates from Maldon and other East Coast ports as required. Bookings are taken to sail on board *Repertor* during races.

**Web site** - *www.repertor.com*

**Matches entered 2016**
Medway 3rd, Pin Mill, Retired, Swale 3rd, Colne 3rd
**Position in Class**
Equal third
**Over all Championship position**
Equal eleventh

**Matches entered 2015**
Medway, Unplaced, Pin Mill 2nd, Swale 3rd, Thames 4th, Colne, Unplaced
**Position in Class**
Fourth
**Over all Championship position**
Equal seventh

**Matches entered 2014**
Medway 3rd, Blackwater 3rd, Pin Mill 1st Also "Spiro Lang Trophy" for fastest start overall, Swale 3rd, Southend 3rd, Colne 3rd
**Over all Championship position**
Fourth

# BLACKTHORN

## Blackthorn

**Slow Staysail / Coasting Class**

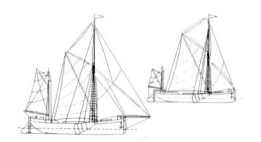

**Construction** - Steel
**Dimensions** - Length 44 ft Beam 12.5 ft
**Bob** - Green and white with red wheat sheaf
**Bowsprit** - No
**Mizzen** - Small
**Davits** - At stern
**Other recognition features** - Cream sprit. Black hull with prominent red and cream trim.

**Notes** - Built in 1993 by Owen Emerson in his yard at Lower Upnor on the River Medway, *Blackthorn* was intended from the outset to be used for recreational purposes rather than as a cargo carrier like the similarly sized *Cygnet*.

Although much of the gear on board *Blackthorn* was either reclaimed from older vessels or constructed to original designs, she has been equipped to give the greatest possible level of comfort and safety as a "Barge yacht". When advertised for sale a few years ago this equipment was described as follows :

*A large galley and saloon area under the main hatch with seating for 6+ around the table, two sofa berths and a wood burning stove. The galley has a large sink and drainer, LPG cooker with a 4-hob burner, grill and oven. There is an LPG Electrolux fridge, pressurised water system and LPG hot water heater. There is a heads with washbasin and a separate bathroom with bath under the mast deck. Blackthorn has two double berths with large drawers beneath and full height wardrobes under the fore hatch.*

Add to this her 120 hp British Leyland engine and you have comfort and convenience which would be unrecognisable to those who earned their living in the barges a hundred years ago.

Based at Iken Cliff on the Alde Estuary near Pin Mill in Suffolk, *Blackthorn* has not been a regular participant in the Barge Matches this Century so it was exciting to see her involved in the Blackwater and Pin Mill events in 2016.

**Matches entered 2016**
Blackwater 2nd Also "Fastest start" Pin Mill, Retired
**Position in Class**
Equal fifth
**Over all Championship position**
Sixteenth

**Matches entered 2015**
None

**Matches entered 2014**
None

**CAMBRIA**

## CAMBRIA of London
*Official number 120676*

**Slow Staysail / Coasting Class**

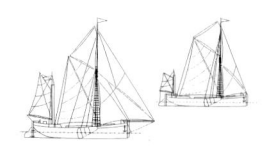

**Construction** - Wood
**Dimensions** - Length 90.95 ft Beam 22 ft
**Bob** - Red, white, blue and green quadrants
**Bowsprit** - Yes
**Mizzen** - Large
**Davits** - At stern
**Other recognition features** - Plain sprit, black top to light grey hull. Has prominent yellow and blue Rotary Club circular logo in Tops'l.
**Notes** - *Cambria* was built by William Eberhardt of Greenhithe in 1906 for the family business. Frederick changed his and the company name to the less Germanic, "Everard" in 1917. *Cambria* spent her early working life doing cross channel trips for Everard's, also building a reputation as a racing barge. *Cambria* remained with F T Everard's until sold to Bob Roberts who had first skippere'd her in 1954. He operated her from 1966 to 1970.

Taken over by The Maritime Trust, *Cambria* moved to St. Katharine's Dock in 1971 where she remained until she was sold to the Cambria Trust for £1. With the aid of an HLF grant restoration was carried out under the leadership of Tim Goldsack at Faversham. *Cambria* returned to sailing in 2011, equipped with streamlined "racing" lee boards which she uses to good effect!

Now working as an education and charter barge sponsored by Rotary Club. *Cambria* is based at Faversham. *Cambria* will continue to contest at least the Medway and Thames Matches where she has such a good record.

**Web site** - *www.cambriabargecharter.co.uk*

**Matches entered 2016**
Medway 1st, Thames 1st Also "Best performing Mainsheetman" - Cyril Varley "Most valued crew member" - Deben Johnson
**Position in Class**
Equal second
**Over all Championship position**
Equal ninth

**Matches entered 2015**
Medway 1st, Thames 3rd, Southend 3rd
**Position in Class**
First
**Over all Championship position**
Equal seventh

**Matches entered 2014**
Medway 1st, Blackwater 3rd
**Over all Championship position**
Tenth

# CENTAUR

## CENTAUR of Harwich
*Official No. 99460*

**Slow Staysail / Coasting Class**

**Construction** - Wood
**Dimensions** - Length 85.54 ft Beam 19.5 ft
**Bob** - Gold wheel on red & black ground
**Bowsprit** - No
**Mizzen** - Small
**Davits** - At stern
**Other recognition features** - Cream sprit with black, cream and red banding. Blue transom.
**Notes** - Built at Harwich in 1895 by John and Herbert Cann, *Centaur* was originally owned by Charles Stone. She passed through several owners but by 1944 she was with Brown and Co. who de-rigged her and used her as a timber lighter. *Centaur* was bought in 1966 by Richard Duke who re-rigged her as a charter barge, selling her in 1974 to the Thames Barge Sailing Club which became a Charitable Trust in 2003 as the Thames Sailing Barge Trust.

Based at Maldon and rebuilt 1984-95, *Centaur* continues to be operated by the Trust along with *S B Pudge*. TSBT is an organisation dedicated to promoting and teaching the practice of the traditional skills of seamanship involved in sailing and maintaining these historic craft.

In 2013-14 *Centaur* had her bottom doubled with the help of an HLF grant. This has enabled her to play a big part in the Sailing Barge Trust's initiative, to recruit and train, approximately ten volunteer "Third Hands" to train as barge crew. Thus passing on the necessary skills to maintain an active fleet in the future.

**Web site** - *www.bargetrust.org*

**Matches entered 2016**
Blackwater, Unplaced, Pin Mill, Unplaced, Swale 3rd, Colne 1st
**Position in Class**
Fourth
**Over all Championship position**
Equal eleventh

**Matches entered 2015**
Medway 3rd, Pin Mill, Retired, Swale 2nd, Thames 4th
**Position in Class**
Fourth
**Over all Championship position**
Eleventh

**Matches entered 2014**
Medway 2nd, Blackwater 1st Also "First round the outer mark", Pin Mill 1st
**Over all Championship position**
Equal sixth

**CYGNET**

## CYGNET of Harwich
*Official No. 84028*

**Slow Staysail / Coasting Class**

**Construction** - Wood
**Dimensions** - Length 41.96 ft Beam 12.98 ft
**Bob** - Red and Blue
**Bowsprit** - Yes
**Mizzen** - Small, stepped on rudder post
**Davits** - Not usually mounted
**Other recognition features** - Plain brown sprit, black hull has prominent pale blue topping. Large steering tiller.
**Notes** - Built in 1881 by Curel, *Cygnet*, unlike the other diminutive barges *Blackthorn* and *Dinah*, was built as a working barge for use trading to small farms and creeks on the Suffolk and Essex marshes. First owned by Walter Wrinch of Ewarton, near Shotley, she stayed with the same family transporting farm produce until the end of the Second World War.

In 1945 *Cygnet* took on a new role, when, in the ownership of a Mr E Mumford she had her sailing gear replaced by two petrol engines and she moved to Foulness carrying cockle shells for chicken grit. Owners at Leigh on Sea in Essex and Queenborough in Kent followed.

Mica Brown acquired *Cygnet* in 1988, refitting her as a private yacht barge. With full sailing gear. In 2004 she had a tiller fitted in place of her wheel. This and her mizzen stepped on the rudder post gives *Cygnet* a distinctive look.

*Cygnet's* can frequently be seen being sailed single handedly around the East Coast by her current Skipper, Des Kaliszewski. When not sailing *Cygnet* is usually based on the Alde, either at Iken Cliff or at Pin Mill.

**Matches entered 2016**
Blackwater 1st Also "First round the outer mark"
**Position in Class**
Equal fifth
**Over all Championship position**
Fifteenth

**Matches entered 2015**
Blackwater 1st Also "First round the outer mark"and "Fastest start"
**Position in Class**
Fifth
**Over all Championship position**
Twelfth

**Matches entered 2014**
Pin Mill 3rd Also award for "Overall excellence"
**Over all Championship position**
Equal eighteenth

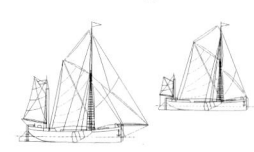

# DEFIANCE

Photo courtesy of Phillip Apps

## DEFIANCE of London
Official No. 917888

**Slow Staysail / Coasting Class**

**Construction** - Wood
**Dimensions** - Length 78 ft   Beam 17.8 ft
**Bob** - Yellow crescent, red sun yellow star within, on a blue background with red ends
**Bowsprit** - No
**Mizzen** - Small,
**Davits** - At stern
**Other recognition features** - Cream sprit with broad blue band. Grey hull with black top and lee boards.
**Notes** - *Defiance* was built by Lambon Hull Ltd, of Rushock, Worcestershire, in 2008. Taken by low loader to Tilbury, she was launched by crane and tugged round to Allington Lock, Maidstone, where she was initially based.

Owner Philip Apps spent the next two years working on, *Defiance* which also spent a year at Stargate Marina where she was shortened by 300 mm. Major adjustments were also made to gain more run on the bow and stern.

*Defiance* was built on the lines of a River Barge, most of which, not having to cope with heavy seas, do not have much sheer, (*Lady of the Lea* has a similar flat profile). She was named after the Hudson's of Maidstone built *Defiance* (Off. No 26241) of 1789. Much of the equipment on *Defiance* has been "recycled" from other barges. The steering gear from *Lady Helen,* wheel, windless and lee boards from *Jock,* main brail winch from *Felix, s*ome rigging from *Dawn* and a top cap from *Niagara!*

Now based at Hoo, *Defiance* has had new metal lee boards fitted during the Winter of 2015/6, replacing her old wooden ones. *Defiance* is used for recreational sailing and has been fitted out for living aboard.

*Defiance* has not yet been regularly used for racing but did have a sail round for the Whitstable Harbour Match in 2015 where she came in fourth. She also attended the Southend event in the same year. She made her Championship debut in 2016 when she came Second in her Class at Southend.

**Matches entered 2016**
Southend 2nd
**Position in Class**
Equal seventh
**Over all Championship position**
Equal Seventeenth

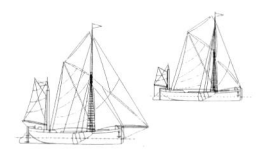

**DINAH**

## DINAH of Rochester
*Official No. 090995*

**Slow Staysail / Coasting Class**

**Construction** - Wood
**Dimensions** - Length 45 ft Beam 12 ft
**Bob** - Red and White
**Bowsprit** - No
**Mizzen** - Small, stepped on rudder post
**Davits** - Not usually carried
**Other recognition features** - Red trim fore and aft, tiller steered
**Notes** - Like *Blackthorn, Dinah* was never intended to carry cargo. She was built by Gill and sons of Rochester in 1887 as a 45 ft barge yacht for The Hon. Reginald Brougham, inventor of the metal golf wood. By 1916 however, her Merchant Navy List entry rather grandly lists her owner as "Ernest Cecil Latter Baillie, Corinthian Club, Piccadilly, London". Originally spritsail rigged and registered at only 19 tons she is shown in the MNL of 1916 as being in the service of Howard Hollingsworth of North Lowestoft.

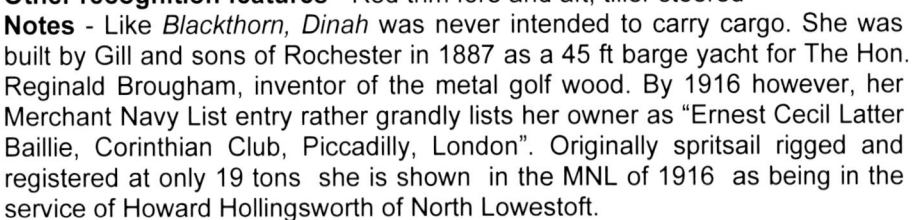

*Dinah* was subsequently converted to a gaff rig and is known to have had a tall mainmast and topmast with a standing gaff and no bowsprit when she was taken to Whitehouse Boatyard at Hoo in 1947. Major work was undertaken including replacing her old paraffin engine with a Ford V 8.

In 1979 Aidan de la Mare rescued her from a lighter in Gloucester where she had become derelict. *Dinah* was taken to Dock End Yard in Ipswich for major refurbishment work which was started but not finished.

In 2003 Richard Johnson had her totally restored in Southwold by a traditional boat builder. Three years of work on the restoration was aided by three generations – Grandfather 84, son 50 and grandson 20 years old.

*Dinah* has now been fully restored and operates from Iken Barns in Suffolk and is only a very occasional Barge Match competitor.

**Matches entered 2016**
None

**Matches entered 2015**
Colne 1st Also "Seamanship" award
**Position in Class**
Seventh
**Over all Championship position**
Equal fifteenth

**Matches entered 2014**
Blackwater, Unplaced, Also "Fastest start"
**Over all Championship position**
Twenty first

# LADY DAPHNE

**LADY DAPHNE of Rochester**  **Slow Staysail /**
*Official No. 127276*  **Coasting Class**

**Construction** - Wood
**Dimensions** - Length 90.8 ft Beam 21.4 ft
**Bob** - Blue and red
**Bowsprit** - No
**Mizzen** - Small
**Davits** - At stern
**Other recognition features** -White Z in topsail. Plain cream sprit
**Notes** - *Lady Daphne* was built in 1923 by Short Bros. of Rochester for David J Bradley. operating under sail alone until receiving an auxiliary engine in 1932.

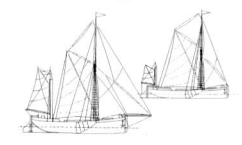

    R & W Paul (Maltsters) Ltd of Ipswich bought *Lady Daphne* in 1937, replacing her old engine with a Ruston and Hornsby motor in 1947. Ten years later sail gave way to power completely and she became a motor barge.

    In 1973. She was sold to Taylor Woodrow Property Ltd who re-rigged her for charter and promotional work.

    In 1996 ownership passed to Elisabeth and Michael Mainelli who operate *Lady Daphne* as a fifty four passenger corporate entertainment and charter barge from St Katharine's Dock under the banner of Nymph Ltd. and Classic Boat Charter. Charters available include passing through Tower Bridge, for which the bridge is of course raised!

    *Lady Daphne*, has undergone a steady program of restoration. Her steering gear was overhauled at Faversham in 2009/10. In 2011 she had a new midship section, portside framing and planking and the starboard side wale replaced. She also had improvements to the galley, heads and fo'cs'le.

    At the time of writing, *Lady Daphne* is for sale. Her owners tell us that any buyer will be encouraged to race her now that repair work has been undertaken on the hole in her hull which prevented racing in 2016.
**Web site** - *www.lady-daphne.co.uk*

**Matches entered 2016**
None

**Matches entered 2015**
Medway 2nd, Thames 2nd
**Position in Class**
Equal second
**Over all Championship position**
Equal ninth

**Matches entered 2014**
Southend 2nd
**Over all Championship position**
Equal fifteenth

# LADY OF THE LEA

## LADY OF THE LEA of Dover
*Official No. 722956*

**Slow Staysail / Coasting Class**

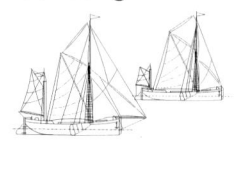

**Construction** - Wood
**Dimensions** - Length 72 ft Beam 13 ft
**Bob** - Plain red.
**Bowsprit** - Yes
**Mizzen** - Small
**Davits** - Not usually carried
**Other recognition features** -Brown sprit with grey band. Has white barge inside castle, all inside double circle emblem, in topsail

**Notes** - *Lady of the Lea* was built in 1931 by Hyam & Oliver at Rotherhithe as a "War Department Sailing Barge", originally being stumpy rigged and tiller steered. Her early duties were to carry armaments between Waltham Abbey and Woolwich Arsenal. Making part river and part canal journeys she was often powered by horse as well as sail! (The Navy added a petrol engine in 1943).

The Royal Gunpowder Mills at Waltham Abbey have a diorama showing *Lady of the Lea* at work loading up to 500 barrels of gunpowder for each cargo.

She was sold to W Aslett in 1946 and subsequently to her present owner Brian Pain. *Lady of the Lea* was largely rebuilt between 1980 and 1990 including doubling her bottom and lower hull.

She returned to the River Lea in the Autumn of 2009 being featured on a BBC Television programme on the area. Privately owned, she is now based at Standard Quay Faversham.

**Matches entered 2016**
Medway, Retired but "First across the start line", Thames 2nd Also "Achievement" award, Swale 1st Also "Fastest start for barge in class", Southend 1st Also "Fastest start for barge in class"
**Position in Class**
First
**Over all Championship position**
Fourth
**Matches entered 2015**
Medway, Unplaced, Swale 3rd, Thames 1st
**Position in Class**
Equal second
**Over all Championship position**
Equal ninth

**Matches entered 2014**
Swale 2nd Also "First round the outer mark in class", Southend 1st Also "Fastest start over all"
**Over all Championship position**
Eighth

# ORINOCO

# ORINOCO of London

**Slow Staysail / Coasting Class**

**Construction** - Wood
**Dimensions** - Length 86 ft Beam 21.5 ft
**Bob** - Plain dark green
**Bowsprit** - No
**Mizzen** - Small
**Davits** - At stern
**Other recognition features** - Sprit brown with white/black/white banding. White ball in Tops'l

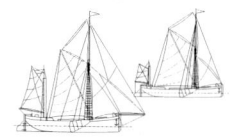

**Notes** - Built by Hughes at East Greenwich in 1895 *Orinoco* was originally owned by Masons the cement makers. She passed to Cranfield Bros, possibly when Masons ceased trading in 1907. When sold to Cranfield's *Orinoco* had a white ball emblem in her tops'l, this motif was subsequently adopted by the Company!

Cranfield's fitted her with a Ruston Auxiliary engine in 1947 and continued using her until she was run down and sunk in the Thames Estuary in 1966. *Orinoco* was repaired and re-rigged by Chester Lighterage and subsequently operated privately by their owner. More problems followed in 1977 when she ran aground, having dragged her anchor in a storm. It took six months to re-float her. She was then sold to Roger Popp and Peter Sands, the present owner of *Niagara*, who raced her successfully.

Bought by her present owner Geoffrey Ingle in 1998, *Orinoco* is now based at Faversham where she undergoes a continuing program of restoration. This has included the re-fitting of her original 1895 ships wheel which was in the care of the Royal Harwich Yacht Club for many years.

Not a regular competitor, *Orinoco* usually contests her local Swale Match.

**Matches entered 2016**
Swale 2nd
**Position in Class**
Equal seventh
**Over all Championship position**
Equal seventeenth

**Matches entered 2015**
Swale 1st Also "First round the outer mark in class"
**Position in Class**
Sixth
**Over all Championship position**
Equal thirteenth

**Matches entered 2014**
Swale 1st Also "Fastest start in class"
**Over all Championship position**
Equal twelfth

**PUDGE** *Dunkirk Little Ship*

## PUDGE of Rochester
*Official No. 127274*

**Slow Staysail / Coasting Class**

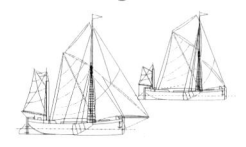

**Construction** - Wood
**Dimensions** - Length 82.36 ft Beam 20.98 ft
**Bob** - Gold wheel emblem on red & black ground
**Bowsprit** - No
**Mizzen** - Small,
**Davits** - At stern
**Other recognition features** - Sprit cream with blue and red bands. Thin white line round top of hull below gunwales. Thin yellow arrow arrow above white line pointing to green flashing at bow.
**Notes** - *Pudge* was built 1922 by the London & Rochester Trading Co. She worked for this Company until being requisitioned in 1940 for Operation Dynamo, in which she is credited with the rescue of over three hundred servicemen from the Dunkirk beaches. In 2015 *Pudge* returned to Dunkirk as part of the commemoration of the seventy fifth anniversary of Operation Dynamo.

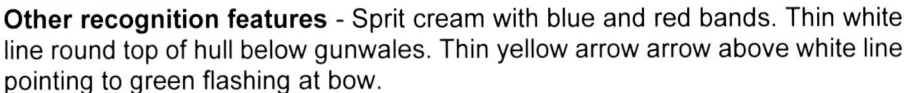

After the war *Pudge* continued "In Trade", now as a motor barge, until bought and re-rigged by the Thames Barge Sailing Club (now Trust) in 1968.

A staged programme of renewal and restoration began in 2005. *Pudge* returned to full operational sailing in 2012. The Barge Trust continues fund raising towards the completion of the work. It is anticipated that the next phase of which should begin in 2017. This and her operations aimed at preserving and teaching the skills needed to sail and maintain the traditions of the working sailing barge, determines her availability to compete in Matches.

**Web site** - *www.bargetrust.org*

**Matches entered 2016**
Medway 2nd Also "First to outer mark in class" and "Seamanship" award, Blackwater 3rd , Pin Mill 3rd
**Position in Class**
Equal second
**Over all Championship position**
Equal ninth

**Matches entered 2015**
Colne, Retired
**Position in Class**
Eighth
**Over all Championship position**
Eighteenth

**Matches entered 2014**
Blackwater, Unplaced, Swale 3rd, Southend, Retired
**Over all Championship position**
Fourteenth

# THALATTA

## THALATTA of Harwich
Official No.116179

**Slow Staysail / Coasting Class**

**Construction** - Wood
**Dimensions** - Length 88.9 ft Beam 20.6 ft
**Bob** - Red with ECST in white
**Bowsprit** - Yes
**Mizzen** - Large
**Davits** - Amidships
**Other recognition features** - Sprit light tan. White "Aspinall" sponsors logo in tops'l. Blue transom

**Notes** - Built at Harwich by W B McLearon and bought by F W Horlock *Thalatta* was launched in February 1906. Briefly spritsail rigged she was soon changed to a ketch rig as this was more suitable for her coastal and cross channel work.

*Thalatta* was sold to the Wynnfield Shipping Company in 1917 and was sold again in 1923, this time to Herbert Body who returned her to a spritsail rig. Purchased by R W Paul's in 1933, *Thalatta* was fitted with a diesel engine in 1947, remaining as a motor barge until 1966. In that year John Kemp bought her and with Jane Benham re-fitted and re-rigged her as a "Mulie" for sail training, thus making her the first Thames sailing barge in this role.

In 1971 *Thalatta* was taken over by the newly formed East Coast Sail Trust who continued her work providing cruises for children.

After nearly a hundred years of continuous sailing, *Thalatta* underwent a thorough refurbishment at St. Osyth Boatyard from 2005 to 2012. The significance of her work with schools and her historic importance was recognised in the scale of the support for this project received from HLF.

*Thalatta* is based at Ipswich during the sailing season and under cover at Heybridge Lock in the winter.

The nature of her work with children for the East Coast Sail Trust means that *Thalatta* is only likely to be seen taking part in an occasional Match as her work and maintenance schedules permit.

*Thalatta* now carries the logo of Aspall, the Suffolk cider makers who have recently become one of her sponsors.

**Web site** - *www.thalatta.org.uk*

**Matches entered 2016**
None

**Matches entered 2015**
None

**Matches entered 2014**
Southend 3rd
**Over all Championship position**
Equal eighteenth

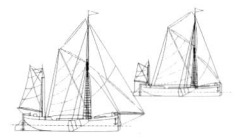

# Following the Matches

Without doubt the best way to watch a Barge Match is from the water. Some competing barges carry fare paying passengers giving an excellent opportunity to soak up the atmosphere of the race.

For those wishing to get a close up view of all the barges, a trip on a vessel following a Match is ideal. Unlike competing barges, vessels following Matches can manoeuvre through the field to get the best views of all the participants.

Others may sometimes be available but the following historic vessels regularly follow one or more of the Barge Matches.

### S.B. Hydrogen

Built in 1906 by Gills of Rochester, at 94.75 ft long *Hydrogen* is the largest wooden barge still sailing. She now works as a charter barge carrying up to fifty passengers for her owners Topsail Charters.

*www.top-sail.co.uk*

### S.B. Kitty

Built of wood at Harwich in 1895 by J H Cann, *Kitty* has at various times defied U boats taking coal to France in WWI, been a timber lighter and a floating restaurant! She now operates as a charter barge, usually from Maldon.

*www.sailingbargekitty.com*

### S.B. Thistle

Built in 1895 at Port Glasgow, *Thistle* is the oldest surviving iron barge and the only one to have been built in Scotland. Like *Hydrogen*, *Thistle* operates as a fifty place charter barge for Topsail Charters of Maldon.

*www.top-sail.co.uk*

### S.B. Victor

Built of in 1895 by Shrubsall's of Ipswich, Victor has served as a munitions carryer, a motor barge, a strip club, a houseboat and now a 40 place charter barge based in Mistley!

*www.sbvictor.co.uk*

### X Pilot

A 72 ton 62 feet long, ex pilot vessel. Built in 1967, and now working as a charter vessel, *X Pilot* is involved with *Project Redsand* to restore one of the Thames Estuary forts. She follows some Barge Matches in the Kent area.

More modern, The *MV Pocahontas,* based at Gravesend is a 110 foot Motor Vessel which follows some barge Matches when other commitments allow.

*www.princess-pocahontas.com*

# Smack Racing

Although there is no championship for Fishing Smacks in the way that there is for Thames sailing barges, several races take place each year coordinated by the Sailing Smack Association. (SSA) Some of these races are held in conjunction with, or at least, at the same time as, Barge Matches. The following events usually have Smacks competing on the same day -

Blackwater
Swale
Colne

For those interested in seeing Smacks and Bawleys being put through their paces there are a number of other events which may be of interest -

**Old Gaffers Association Brightlingsea Rally**
*www.oldgaffersassociation.org*
**Pin Mill smack race** - usually held separately from the Barge match.
*www.pmsc.org.uk*
**Rowhedge Regatta** *www.rowhedge-regatta.co.uk*
**Heybridge Basin Regatta** *www.heybridgebasinregatta.co.uk*
**Whitstable barge and smack race** - No official web site at time of writing but information can sometimes be found at the web site of sailing barge *Greta*.
*www.greta1892.co.uk*
**Mersea week and Mersea Town Regatta** *www.mersearegatta.org.uk*
**Mersea Oyster Dredging match** *www.mersearegatta.org.uk*
**Maldon Town Regatta** *www.maldonregatta.co.uk*

The Blackwater Smack Race usually starts immediately after the Barge Match. *Sunbeam* nearest the camera just ahead passing Stansgate.

# Acknowledgements and Bibliography

We would like to acknowledge the tremendous contribution made by many people in the compilation not only of this book but the others in the *Illustrated guide to* - series.

In the compilation of this book we would like to particularly thank Paul Jeffies of *Topsail Charters* for his tremendous technical assistance on matters relating to the sailing of barges under racing conditions and for supplying the dates of the next two years Barge Matches.

The untiring research of Chris Kite, Historian and contributor to the Autumn 2016 edition of *Mainsheet*, the magazine of the *Society for Sailing Barge Research* enabled us (we hope) to avoid some of the pitfalls when it came to outlining the history and origins of the first sailing barge "Match".

We would also like to thank Steve, of *North Sea Sails* in Tollesbury for background information on sails he has made for many of the barges in this book. Not all of this information has found its way into these pages but it has proved invaluable in helping to understand other information given to us.

## Bibliography

***The Illustrated Guide to Thames sailing barges,*** (*Eighth Edition*) Phillips Design Publishing- ISBN 9780.0.99356692.0.3 - Illustrates and describes all the currently active fleet, restorations and static examples. Includes interesting features.

***Sailing a Thames Barge, sail by sail*** - (Via Thames Barge Sailing Trust) P. Hearn. Now updated by Andrew Berry. "Which rope to pull, why to pull it what it does and when" on *S B Pudge*.

***The Racing Horlocks 1968-1971*** - (from SSBR) Ron Weyda with Bob Horlock.

***The Thalatta Diaries*** - Heritage House (Publishing) Ltd, R Phillips ISBN1.85215.1811 Amusing and entertaining account of life and work with children on a Sailing barge in the early 21st century.

***Sailing barge compendium*** - Compiled by John White. ISBN 9780950051574 Available from SSBR.

**The following web sites may be of use or interest-**

**www.adls.org.uk** Association of Dunkirk Little Ships.
**www.bargetrust.org** Charity for the preservation and sailing of Thames barges.
**www.merseamuseum.org.uk** Has Mercantile Navy Lists of various years. A fascinating glimpse into the past. Use official numbers to check barge identities as often more than one barge is listed with the same name.
**www.nationalhistoricships.org.uk** National Historic Ships site. Their "Register" section is invaluable in the preparation of this book.
**www.sailingbargeassociation.co.uk** Organisers of the Barge matches, Check on individual matches here before travelling.
**www.sailingbargeresearch.org.uk** The Society for Sailing Barge Research. A must for everyone with an interest in the historical aspects of the barges.
**www.thamesbarge.org.uk** - Barge news.